DRIVE IT!

Drive It!

A GOLFER'S GUIDE TO GREATER DISTANCE & CONTROL WITH THE TOUGHEST CLUB IN THE BAG

FRANK GROVES

BURFORD BOOKS

Printed in the United States of America.

10 9 8 7 6 5 4 3 2 1

Library of Congress Cataloging-in-Publication Data
Groves, Frank.
    Drive it! / Frank Groves.
        p. cm.
    ISBN 1-58080-116-1 (pbk.)
1. Golf—Drive. I. Title.
    GV979.D74G76 2003
    796.352'3—dc21
                                        2003012678

Contents

Prologue: Calvin

Calvin spotted me hitting practice balls at Pinehurst on a spring evening in '69. Very nearly broke, sleeping in my old Plymouth Comet parked behind the Holiday Inn, I had just squeaked through qualifying for the North-South Amateur with a 74 on the number 5 course. With the draft looming close, I had incredibly left Michigan's engineering school in my last semester, scrounged up what little cash I had left from what seemed like about fifteen different part-time jobs, and driven south. Pairings had just been announced for the next day's first-round matches. I had drawn Ed Tutwiler, Walker Cup team member and runner-up in the U.S. Amateur.

With the pressure of qualifying behind me, all the improvements recently made in my swing fell into place. Shot after shot streaked dead onto the flag in the practice fairway. After a while I noticed an old black gentleman, probably one of the Pinehurst caddies, who was standing some ten yards behind watching me hit. Looking for a bag for the tournament, I thought, *He'd do better finding someone who could pay him.* Continuing to hit, I could feel him closing in.

"Man, you hittin' that ball nice," he said. "Got a caddy?" He had a bowling ball for a head with a good bit of gray on top, kindly eyes, a nose that looked like it had been in a few fights in its younger days, and a permanent smile. At sixty, he looked like he could still play linebacker.

"No," I said, "thanks. Think I'll carry them myself."

"You hittin' it good enough to win, young man," he persisted, "but you not gonna win without a good caddy. I'm a good one. Carried for Hogan. Carried for Snead. Know a good swing when I see it. You can win here, but you need a caddy who knows the place." He stuck out his hand. "Calvin's my name," he said.

Well, in the end there was no use arguing with him. I let him hit a few balls while I rested, hoping he would give up and leave. He had a swing like Mike Souchak's, one of the purest I ever saw. I told him I couldn't afford a caddy. Didn't faze him. When he persisted, I confessed to sleeping in the car. That just made him mad.

"Man," he said, "what you wanna go do that for. Cain't win sleepin' in a damn car! Here's the deal," he concluded. "You comin' back with me and sleepin' in a bed. I'm gonna caddy for you and we gonna win this tournament!"

Driving into North Carolina, I had passed a lot of shanties with about half a dozen rusting cars and twice as many kids in the front yards. The Comet was beginning to seem more attractive.

"I can't impose on your family, Calvin," I said.

"I'm not talkin' about my house," he said. "I'm porter at the Old Magnolia Inn here in town. Some nights I sleep there on a bed in the back room. You sleep there, I sleep at home. No problem."

So I moved into the Old Magnolia that night. The owners, who acted like Calvin was director of the inn, adopted me even worse than Calvin had. Set me a place at the evening table with their guests and started laying odds on my chances with Tutwiler.

In the morning I hit the ball so well in practice that, when I shook hands with my opponent on the first tee, I thought, *He is not going to know what hit him.* Calvin handed me the driver and said, "Left center"—like he was ordering a sandwich. When I birdied two of the first three, Calvin said, "Don't go soft on this guy. Put him away!"

We won the match 5 and 4. Back at the inn that night I was a hero, the cause célèbre of the owners and guests. The next day several of them followed us around as we beat Bob Zender, 3 and 2. Zender, a big-hitting college all-American, outdrove me by thirty yards, but each time he pulled out his short iron for the approach, he'd be staring at my 3-iron shot sitting next to the flag. Calvin took all this for granted like it was preordained. Me, I just took the club and did what Calvin told me to do.

The next day we beat Bud Stevens, many-time Michigan amateur champ. It was a tight match all the way. Calvin kept saying, "Gonna be a tough one. Just gotta wear him down." Each time I wanted to get too aggressive, Calvin backed me off. We got to eighteen 1 up. I gagged my uphill way on the difficult par 4 for a bogey 5 and Bud drove into the rough and bogeyed it, too. Three matches down, three to go.

The next day I ruined Calvin's script when I argued with him and went my own way on the second shot to the fourteenth. I had never heard of Jim Gabrielson (Walker Cup veteran) in those days, so for once I didn't think of myself as the underdog. Standing in the fairway at fourteen, we were dead even. We had been even all day, in fact, since we'd both parred every hole. The flag was back on the Donald Ross domed green. Calvin handed me a 4-iron.

"I can't get back to the flag with this," I complained.

"Yeah, I know," he said. "Nothing'll hold back there."

Was it nerves, lack of patience, or arrogance? All of the above, probably. I talked Calvin into an easy 3-iron and, to deaden its landing, cut the sweetest shot you ever saw into a light breeze quartering left and against. Almost hit the flag, barely rolled off the green, and kept on going for about fifteen yards. Bogey. In the end Jim made eighteen pars and I made seventeen pars and one very stupid bogey.

Calvin wasn't even mad at me, just disappointed. He'd seen enough of life to know you don't write your own script, but it still didn't stop him from trying. In fact, he blamed himself for getting talked into that 3-iron by someone forty years his junior.

So I got my tail between my legs, made Calvin accept forty dollars since I had saved some cash sponging meals off the inn—this left me fifty bucks to drive back to Michigan—thanked the folks at Old Magnolia profusely, and drove off to my appointment with Uncle Sam. I might have won that tournament if I'd just kept on listening to Calvin.

I never got back down to Pinehurst. Once I got home I borrowed some money, sent Calvin a decent caddy fee, and wrote a thank-you to the owners of the Old Magnolia Inn. Life moves on. Army, marriage, babies, job, college for the babies. Now I'm nearly as old as Calvin was when he adopted me for a week in '69. Caddies now come with wheels and battery instead of a permanent smile. Wherever you are, Calvin, I'd like to say, "Thank you."

Introduction

G olfers the world over covet that all-too-rare moment of perfect collision of clubhead and ball. A sensual rush blitzes up the synapses from the fingers to the brain. The head rotates and the eyes bring into focus a white ball receding into the blue horizon, streaking dead onto the flagstick. The brain broadcasts the ecstatic message throughout the body: *Perfection!*

The intensity of pure impact with the golf ball is reflected by the richness of the slang surrounding the event. He crushed it. She flushed it. He creamed, smacked, clobbered, murdered, nailed, drilled, hammered, animalized, ripped, and pured it. This plenitude of strange verbs attempts to describe the indescribable and is perhaps exceeded in number and richness only by the slang surrounding the act of reproduction. In each case our species, the most evolved (we like to think) interpretation of carbon-based life, is dumbfounded by the mystery and sensation of the event.

"Why can't I hit a driver? I hit my short irons okay and am usually pretty good with the 3 wood, but I stink with the driver!"

This golfer's lament drives a booming business in bizarre-looking drivers. Engineers study bell curves showing the distribution of bad golf swings with specific characteristics, then build computer models of the most common flawed swings. How can you turn a spun-out, cut-across swipe at the golf ball with a clubface that isn't square into a long and straight hit? The short answer, of course, is that it cannot consistently be done. But if you build a driver with a huge head and sweet spot and a closed face, then mount it on a whippy shaft so that the clubface can briefly ignore all the bad instructions being transmitted from the golfer's hands just prior to impact, you can make some bad drives turn out better. Then if you construct the thing from unobtainium, you can get seven hundred bucks for a club that costs you fifty dollars to make, become rich, and live happily ever after.

Perhaps even better, you can coin a catchy slogan for a seriously flawed set of instructions, do a great job of marketing, and get rich while harming your customers. In a curious way, you can gain job security from your own incompetence. Like the patients of an inept psychiatrist, your pupils grow ever more dependent. All that is needed is to stay one step ahead with a new slogan and another flawed approach.

Have you ever marveled at the great variety of golf swings that make money on the various tours? Does this seem a bit inconsistent with the doctrine of the perfect swing? Can there be only one right way when a Miller Barber or Jim Furyk demolishes a field full of classic swingers on a good weekend? The average Joe golfer subscribes to *Golf Magazine*, reads all the tips, tries to take a logical approach to a bewildering game. He takes lessons from the local pro and wears out grips and hands—only to become worse.

When I'm paired with a struggling mediocre player and have the kind of ball-striking day that inspires my companion to ask for advice, I try to assess just how badly my advice is going to ruin the rest of his or her day before obliging. So rarely does this advice help, especially while on the course, that almost all golfers are quite eager to help their opponents, especially if a few bucks hang in the balance.

Walk into any golf pro shop or, even better, a golf superstore and behold the number of books, tapes, and gadgets targeted at the ever-hopeful golfer. This activity has led me to postulate a theorem; it goes like this: *The number of instruction manuals on a subject is inversely proportional to their effectiveness taken as a whole.* For example, consider diet books. It is about as likely that a fat person will lose one hundred pounds and keep them off as it is that the average golfer will be aided by the majority of these golf instruction devices.

Is there some sort of conspiracy at work within the golf community mandating that every snippet of valid advice must be surrounded with a double helping of contradictory nonsense? Or is it that our unquenchable thirst for the quick-and-easy fix ensures that another new miracle of revolutionary theory will soon be enjoying its brief and counterproductive, yet profitable, day in the sun? Although many wonderful golf instruction books have been produced by the greatest players of all time, the valuable tips and lessons in these books are tossed into a giant stew pot along with the above-mentioned double helping of erroneous information. And there is no divine golfing authority to guide the pupil away from attractive-looking chunks of very bad advice.

Golf is not easy. *Roget's Thesaurus* should add the word *golf* as another of the antonyms of *easy*. And yet the books produced by the top players insist that it's really not a difficult thing to do. Right! Just spend half your waking hours on the course, practice until your hands bleed, and still miss the cut many times a year . . . and then tell a person with just five hours a week for golf that it should be easy.

Golfers are incurable optimists with ever-present expectations of imminent doom. In a just world there would be a better way to instruct these martyrs and reward them a little bit for their heroic tenacity. In this book I put forward the idea that the road to better golf lies not in metaphysical speculation about the angle of the wrist at the top or the amount of extension at takeaway or any of the other seemingly endless number of swing clues that only vaguely pertain to striking the golf ball. It's my idea that the path to better golf begins with an understanding of and physical sensation for what happens at impact in a properly struck golf ball.

My favorite case of incurable golf optimism (and the agony that accompanies constant disillusionment) was my uncle Dubby. Dubby has been gone for seventeen years, yet I have no doubt that—were he brought back to life in good form—he would soon be on the practice tee at the Quincy Country Club trying to cure his slice. Dubby was a good athlete (played basketball at Illinois) and an 8 to 10 handicapper in his best years. He had an excellent short game, hit his irons pretty well, and was a big strong man. Nonetheless, I doubt that he ever flew a drive more than 220 yards and always with a more or less pronounced slice. This slice seriously tainted his quest for happiness on earth. Although Dubby was proud of my early golf successes, I suspect he hated being outdriven by an eleven-year-old. He would have traded many of his earthly possessions for a drive long and straight.

If I happened to find a resurrected Dubby on that practice tee, I think now I could help him. Seldom in his first lifetime did he make truly solid contact with the golf ball. Dubby had a decent grip (a bit too strong) and decent posture (a bit too hunched and rounded at the shoulders), and he reached for the ball too much. Nonetheless, his fundamentals in the above-mentioned categories were not much worse than, say, Craig Stadler. So why does one man win the Masters and another almost never make truly solid contact? *Like so many frustrated golfers, Dubby never learned to attack the ball with the clubhead coming along the inside path just prior to impact.* His natural athletic skills could produce decent iron shots despite this swing fault, but with the longer shaft of the driver, no hand miracle at impact could rescue him from the slice.

The only true contact we have with the golf ball (despite all the theories and begging, swearing, sniveling, and cajoling) is when we hit it. Although the ball stays on the clubface only milliseconds, we have a good sense of whether it is glory or ridicule that awaits the shot by the time the ball is in flight by itself. In those milliseconds a feeling is transmitted up the shaft, through the hands, to the brain and the soul. The moment before impact,

FIGURE 1: THE SECRET OF POWER

a: power stored   **b**: power being unleashed

optimism reigns. How long does it take to sense a shank, a scull, a chunk, a duck hook, a whiff, a topped shot, a pop-up, or ball struck so perfectly that the only thing left to do is pose? It's over in those milliseconds when the hands and arms have either directed the clubhead in a true enough path to find the sweet spot or have managed to put the ball God-knows-where.

Dubby never found the path to the sweet spot often enough for it to become familiar and recognizable. At impact he was always, even in his best swings, swiping across the ball in a more or less weakened and broken-down manner. In any shot longer than thirty to fifty yards this would be the case. As I mentioned above, Dubby never learned to attack the golf ball along the inside-out path, and he never got anywhere near the correct position at impact.

Every very good golfer who has ever played the game has gotten into positions just prior to impact very similar to those shown in the frames of figure 1. The essential secret of power golf is revealed in these photos:

1. Right elbow nearly on right hip.
2. Retained wrist cock until just prior to impact.
3. Clubhead on a distinctly inside-out path.
4. Weight transferred to left foot.
5. Clubhead chases down the target line after impact.

c: power stored **d**: power being unleashed

The swing path that you take starting at address and takeaway matters not at all if you can get into this balanced and powerful position in the impact zone. The conventional approach to golf instruction will have you memorizing a hundred little details that are characteristic of good swings, but you may be left in the dark physically and intellectually regarding the most important detail of all: the correct positions of body and clubhead through the impact zone. *Immediately after teaching grip and posture, golf instruction should go directly to the ingraining of the correct impact zone positions.*

Assuming I could convince Uncle Dubby to endure the ignominy of returning to the most fundamental aspects of the game, I would start with chips and short pitches, which he hit pretty well. We would work to recognize the impact zone body and hand positions that result in a square and descending blow (Dubby, like the vast majority of golfers, tended to pick or sweep the golf ball into flight) to the very back of the golf ball, with the clubhead traveling straight down the line to the target. We would work on the position of the hands, arms, and entire body at impact for these short shots until his brain and his very being learned to recognize the desired positions and the feeling associated with a true hit. Eventually the body learns the correct, inside path to the position at impact and instinctively seeks it out on every shot. Once found, this sense of pure impact is gradually learned for longer and longer shots.

As the swing lengthens, the task becomes more difficult. Countless golfers can strike a short iron reasonably well but are hopeless with a driver. It is obvious that the longer club and swing present a greater challenge, but there seems to be a lack of logical continuity. Golfers who can hit a 5-iron well 50 percent of the time should be able to hit a driver well at least 25 percent of the time. But many times these poor souls have almost never in their lifetimes made really good contact with the driver. How can this be?

As the golf swing proceeds from the putt to ever-longer swings, culminating in the drive, there is a gradual transition from a practical, rational learning method (*I hit the putt fifteen feet too far, thus I hit it too hard*) to a religious mysticism with almost no rational correlation (*I sliced that drive because I did not extend enough on the backswing and went over the line at the top and didn't shift my weight plus I moved my head).* In the first case, the focus is on what happened when the club-head struck the ball and what the golfer did to it at impact. In the second instance, we actually seem to expect that the poor bloke who just hit it out of bounds is going to miraculously correct all of the above imperfections on his next swing. We even imply if he does not fix each and every one of the issues mentioned, he will not have a chance. It is a convincing witness to sheer human stubbornness that this golfer will listen intently, screw up his face in desperate concentration, and give it another whack.

The complexity of the physics of the golf swing coupled with the great diversity in outward appearance of swings that work quite well drags well-intentioned instructors into a swamp of speculation. Golf pros who struggled through high school physics and trigonometry can be overheard on the lesson tee using words like *torque, momentum,* and *swing plane* as they impart the wisdom of their trade to bewildered hackers. In recent years the PGA has tried hard to arrive at a more "standardized" approach to instruction; the advent of the Golf Channel is a step forward. It is also helpful that today's top players—Woods, Els, Mickelson, Singh, and many others—all have nearly perfect golf swings. Nevertheless, average golfers are still confused about how they should swing the club and remain fertile soil for the planting of silly ideas.

So we are subjected to a parade of "brilliant" new ideas about the swing. *Brilliant* is a word so overused it has lost its meaning. On a recent *Monday Night Football* program, John Madden put his finger on it better than I ever could. John said something like this: "You know, it always gets me to hear that so-and-so is a brilliant coach, a brilliant defensive coordinator, a brilliant this and that. Come on! You became a coach in the first place probably because recess was your best subject."

The golf market is always on the lookout for something new and different to promote to frustrated lovers of the game. Like doomed evolutionary mutations, new concepts of the golf swing are spawned, profitably marketed while doing no good whatsoever, and then flame out to well-deserved obscurity. If P. T. Barnum were alive and well today, he would not be able to resist.

"Horse sense is what a horse has that keeps him from betting on humans," said W. C. Fields. It would be quite difficult to sell a seven-hundred-dollar driver to this same discerning horse!

Ending my tour of duty in the army and failing to get my card at the tour school finals in 1971, I served a brief stint as assistant pro at a country club north of Chicago. It was not your "top-of-the-line" club. At buffet lunches the ladies would stuff their purses with leftover food to be devoured at home. A few of these gals had the same approach toward young assistant pros. Members wandered into the pro shop in search of technology's latest cure for the incurable. My suggestions to potential customers that the better approach would be to fix the swing problem earned me an abrupt invitation from the head pro, who had a family to feed, to practice my salesmanship skills elsewhere.

At the tour school that year in Palm Beach Gardens, an aging Wilson representative told us a story about young Sam Snead. When Sam was first discovered and signed on, someone at Wilson had the bright idea that he could be used for testing new club designs.

"Didn't work worth a damn," the old-timer told us. "No matter what club we gave him, Sam would hit one to the right, one to the left, and all the rest would go right where he wanted."

"Nothing wrong with this club," Sam would say.

The change in technology from Bobby Jones's time to present has resulted in much longer ball striking for the top players. Unfortunately, not much of this increase in length has been transferred to the midhandicapper. Certain of the most commonly repeated truths simply must be obeyed to unlock this new potential. Unavoidably, I must repeat many of the tried-and-true instructions to be found in instruction books dating to Jones's time and before:

- ➤ Keep your head down.
- ➤ Keep your left arm straight.
- ➤ Hit down on the golf ball.
- ➤ Hit through to the target.
- ➤ Play one shot at a time.

The problem lies not with the truth of these or many other of golf's most common mantras, for true they are. The difficulty is that they cannot be tackled one at a time; they arrive like a swarm of wasps. As soon as you swat one of them, another one stings you!

This book has been distilled, following the experienced advice of publisher Peter Burford, from my unpublished three-volume series titled *Golf's Grail*. The golf book market, like the diet book market, has been saturated with advice, much of it contradictory. The skies could part and God himself could tell me the exact truth about the golf swing, but I would still be faced with the daunting task of convincing a cynical crowd of golfers who have been deceived by well-intentioned, false promises once too often.

It is a fascinating game—a teacher of invaluable lessons for living or a complete waste of time, depending upon your point of view. "I would never vote for any man guilty of golf," wrote H. L. Mencken, and we all know what Mark Twain thought of our pastime. I began the game so young, I can neither remember nor conceive of life without it. If, years after I am gone, science figures out how to restore my physical and mental health, such as it was, I will soon be back at it. It may be better to let me lie.

Thanks for reading my book and sharing the passion. Good luck!

Selecting Your Driver

"This new driver is magic!" My buddy Hubris Constant sat on the veranda in the twilight, beer in one hand, cigar in the other, holding forth on the virtues of his new driver. "Four hundred and fifty ccs of four-piece, forged and welded, perimeter-weighted titanium with beta-ti, variable thickness, spring-effect face. I had them set it one degree closed with eighteen-by-eighteen bulge and roll. The ball just leaps off this club-face." I pictured the slashing spasm that Hubie calls his golf swing and marveled once again that he could be a 10 handicap. A former triple-A shortstop with exceptional hand-eye coordination, hands talented enough to overcome the slash, and an awful grip to make fairly consistent, solid contact with the ball. And oh, by the way, he consistently holes putts from anywhere on the green.

"Yeah," Hubie continued, "I spent two weeks getting fit into exactly the right club. The forty-five-inch, boron-laced graphite shaft has a mid bend point and a medium-firm tip stiffness with oversized hosel. It's got a torque of three degrees, frequency matched with my other woods, and I can hit it as hard as I want and it still goes straight!"

It was a lovely California evening and our friend was happy so we did not remind him of the drive he had hit OB forty yards right on the tenth hole.

That was six months ago. Hubie is now a 12 handicapper and trying out new drivers.

Buried in the marketing smoke and mirrors, some very real improvements in golf club technology continue to occur. Unfortunately, the greatest beneficiaries of these changes have been tour and top amateur players who generate sufficient clubhead speed to compress the new balls and spring-face drivers to take advantage of the latest advances in shafting materials and design. The midhandicap golfer has been helped primarily by the concept of perimeter weighting, which spreads out the sweet spot to lessen the distance loss on the bad swings, but has been left behind in the search for greater distance. It is a little like the old saying about the "rich getting richer."

Thirty-five years ago I competed in the NCAA driving contest held during championship week at Fred Waring's Inn at Shawnee-on-the-Delaware. Buoys were positioned in the shallow water of the river to denote an imaginary narrow fairway, and swimmers radioed back where each ball had landed. We were given five balls and had to get three in the "fairway" to qualify. When I managed this with an average distance of 260 yards, it placed me near the top of the field. The river was 305 yards across at that point, and only one young man, Bunky Henry, hit a shot that did not splash. A few weeks ago at age fifty-six, using a Pro V1 and an eight-degree, titanium Big Bertha with a strong-flex graphite shaft, I flew a drive three hundred yards into a slight breeze. The ball was stuck in its own pitch mark, so it was not a roll!

FIGURE 2: SHAFT COMPARISON

a: whippy, high-torque shaft   b: stiff, low-torque shaft

The twentieth- and twenty-first-century evolution of golf club technology has fundamentally altered the way the best players swing. The modern swing not only has fewer moving parts, but is also a much more muscular adventure than the old-time flowing swing. The braced legs, restricted hip turn, and powerful, vertical dropping of the hands into the slot at the start of the downswing are not compatible with a hickory shaft.

To demonstrate the effect of the flexible shaft versus a stiff one, I borrowed the most flexible driver available from the Alisal Ranch Course pro shop. The left-side photos of figure 2 are with this whippy shaft, and the right-side photos are with my Big Bertha with the strong-flex shaft. As I began hitting the whippy-shafted club, every shot was going high left. With some experimentation, I found that a looser, more flowing and rhythmical swing worked better. When I tried casting my hands somewhat early, instead of retaining the wrist cock until later, the whippy club began to produce consistently straight shots.

The greater amount of flex in the whippy shaft is slightly noticeable in frames a and c. In frame c the clubhead has actually caught up and

c: whippy, high-torque shaft   d: stiff, low-torque shaft

overtaken the shaft, causing the shaft to bend in the opposite direction. It appears that this is also true with the stiff shaft, but to a lesser degree. When I tried to use my normal swing with the whippy shaft, this exaggerated overtaking of the clubhead added loft and closed the clubface, causing the high-and-left ball flight. With the whippy shaft, I could not really hit hard and drive through the ball. The difference in my positions near impact is striking. In frame c I'm in a position very much like an old-time pro swinging a wooden shaft. Timing was even more important in those days because of the shaft's flexibility; there was no way to generate maximum clubhead speed and still control the shot.

These photos and discussions illustrate a tricky aspect to proper driver selection. You want to use a club that fits your swing now, today, but doesn't fight against the swing improvements you'd like to make. Some golf professionals and clubmakers will advise you to use as whippy a shaft as you can control with the idea that it will be the most forgiving of your swing faults. This is probably good advice if you are a casual, occasional golfer without the time or inclination to put in the work to improve your swing. It is also probably good advice if you are reaching an age where physical limitations begin to set in.

On the other hand, if you are determined to hit your drives longer by getting into proper position at impact, then the bias should be set the other way around. If you are trying to decide between a flexible and a standard shaft, tend toward the standard. If you are trying to decide between a standard and a stiff, then set the bias toward the stiff. You cannot *really* hit the long ball until you generate enough clubhead speed to take full advantage of the latest technology. And if you pick a shaft that's too whippy, it will limit your ability to generate clubhead speed and maintain control. At first the stiffer shaft may feel somewhat dead by comparison. Your drives may not be quite as long, but they will be straighter. As you make swing improvements, your stronger move into impact will bring that stiffer shaft to life.

If I were writing this book forty years ago, that would have just about done it for a discussion of driver selection. These days the number of choices and the jargon can be extremely confusing. The most thorough technical glossary I have seen can be accessed at www.swingweight.com; click on the glossary section. This Web site also offers reviews of every driver on the market by a spectrum of testers ranging from scratch to high-handicap golfers. There are also very good articles on every aspect of club design and selection. Several of the articles by Jeff Jackson are so well phrased that I have included direct quotes. It's a great place to get educated quickly about the current technology. Just be aware that the emphasis is on fitting your current swing, no matter how flawed, with compensating equipment. This special equipment could make it very hard to improve that swing.

A driver consists of a head, a shaft, and a grip, so let's begin with a brief discussion of the latest technology.

The Driver Head

WOOD VERSUS METAL

Persimmon woods are now as much a relic of the past as hickory shafts. Wooden driver heads do not allow much freedom of design for enlarged sweet spot, relocated center of gravity, or spring effect. Can a person play perfectly good golf with a persimmon-headed driver? Of course! But when was the last time you saw one in a driving contest?

DRIVER HEAD SIZE, LENGTH, AND SPRING EFFECT

The USGA has recently proposed limitations on clubhead size and length, restricting the overall volume to 385 cc (cubic centimeters) and club length to forty-seven inches. Neither clubhead size nor club length is currently limited.

The USGA and the Royal and Ancient Golf Club of St. Andrews have also recently agreed to place a limit on impact rebound efficiency. The rebound velocity is now prohibited from exceeding 83 percent of the clubhead speed on center impact. There are drivers in the marketplace that violate these restrictions. Anxious golf shops will want to clear out this inventory, so beware! The spring effect is achieved by making the face of the metal wood extremely thin so that it deflects and rebounds like a trampoline upon impact. Some forged drivers feature a changing thickness across the face as an attempt to optimize the spring effect. The large clubhead size allows the designer to move the center of gravity of the driver for specific purposes. A lower center of gravity seems to promote higher ball flight and vice versa. And the large head size is used to increase perimeter weighting in an attempt to straighten out off-center hits. The large head also has a greater structural moment of inertia, which slightly reduces twisting upon impact.

Here is what Mr. Jackson has to say about head size:

> OK, so it has been shown that head size has increased in the past twenty years. So what? There is a legitimate playability reason for these larger heads; they allow the club to possess a higher moment of inertia. That is, the larger club head will resist twisting more than smaller head on off-center hits. For all practical purposes, assuming the specifications for the heads are the same, a larger head will not hit the ball any longer when hit on-center. But, the larger heads allow players who may not be as consistent as they would like, to hit better "misses," in effect making them believe they hit the larger-headed clubs farther.
>
> As a (metal)wood head becomes larger, its center of gravity will be moved back away from the face. The will tend to cause shots to fly higher than expected. . . . Manufacturers have thus reduced the lofts on many of their larger-headed drivers as a result. As the 21st century dawns, it's not uncommon to find offerings as low as 6 degrees among popular drivers (for better players). Note that the face angles of 300+cc heads are typically more closed than those of most clubs; this is to assist these larger heads in squaring to the target at impact. Their larger volumes tend to cause their faces to remain open; closed face angles counteract this tendency."[1]

---

[1] Jeff Jackson, www.swingweight.com/clubhead_technology.htm

SPRING EFFECT VERSUS BULGE AND ROLL

As persimmon driver technology evolved in the twentieth century, it became known through trial and error that a driver face with a certain amount of bulge and roll could impart corrective spin to certain types of off-center hits. The bulge is the heel-to-toe curvature, and the roll is the crown-to-sole curvature. The deflection of the thin-faced, trampoline-effect metal driver face works to negate the bulge and roll effectiveness. As an engineer, it's very hard for me to accept claims that a driver face that acts like a trampoline can increase accuracy. Bouncing on a trampoline is great fun until you happen to land off-center and are rocketed off toward disaster. Club designers are experimenting with variable face thicknesses, changing the bulge and roll radii, and increasing perimeter weighting, hoping to find the magic combination.

DRIVER MATERIALS AND FORGED VERSUS CAST

Forged titanium drivers are typically made from four pieces, with the crown, back, and sole being softer, less expensive pure titanium. The face and hosel are generally alloys with 6 percent aluminum and 4 percent vanadium.

Cast drivers are produced typically in two halves using the "lost-wax" investment casting method. Then the halves are welded together. Again, the discussion at swingweight.com is very good:

> There are many types of steel that may be used in casting, 431 and 17-4 being the most common. 431 is a bit softer than 17-4; a higher nickel content makes the latter harder (stronger). 431 is used exclusively in irons and putters; it is not strong enough to make thin-walled metal heads. 17-4 is used in woods, irons, and putters. There are few, if any, golfers who can actually tell the differences in metal hardness in golf clubs; differences are more psychological than in actual feel. The past couple of years have seen the evolution of other metals used to make metal wood heads. Among these which are harder and lighter than 17-4 are

15-5 stainless and maraging steel, a mixture of any number of heat-treated alloys that are stronger and lighter yet. Titanium has its place in casting as well, but it must be cast in a vacuum environment due to the nature of its molecular makeup. Its hardness is very similar to 17-4 stainless; the reason you see many jumbo ti woods is due to titanium's lighter weight and higher strength-to-weight ratio.[2]

In summary, there is one solid reason beyond the marketing hype why larger metal woods made from exotic materials are winning the battle for both tour players and midhandicappers: The intelligent redistribution of the clubhead's weight can provide more consistent distance and accuracy on less-than-perfect hits. Spring-effect drivers can increase top-level golfers' distances by so much that the USGA has been forced to place limits. The jury is still out on the effectiveness of thin-faced, spring-effect designs for average players, but I suspect that further refinements in this technology will eventually reduce the inconsistent ball flight of off-center hits. If so, this approach can benefit golfers of all calibers, since the face can be thinned to match a player's specific swing speed so long as the 83 percent rebound efficiency is not violated.

The Driver Shaft

Selecting the best shaft for your driver is even more confusing than choosing the proper head. The choice of materials seems endless, and there is almost no standardization among manufacturers concerning shaft flex, torque ratings, flex points, and so on. The traditional clubhead weight rating scale—D1, D2, and so on—is a measure of the relative amount of weight of the club that is concentrated in the head. If you replace the steel shaft of a D1 driver with the lightest graphite shaft, you will now have a club that could measure D4.

---

[2] Jeff Jackson, www.swingweight.com/investment_casting2.htm

STEEL VERSUS GRAPHITE

Three arguments are made for installing the more expensive graphite shaft in your driver: lighter weight, better feel, and selectable torque rating. (All these arguments must be taken with a grain of salt considering that Tiger Woods has rewritten the record book using a steel-shafted driver.) A forty-six-inch-long True Temper Dynamic Gold S300 steel driver shaft weighs 127 grams. A competing graphite shafts offering the same stiffness and similar torque rating will range from sixty-two to eighty grams, depending upon the maker. (By comparison, the weight of an oversized metal head tends to be close to two hundred grams.) The center of mass of a graphite-shafted driver will be three to four inches closer to the clubhead and slighty farther behind the clubface than that of the steel-shafted driver. This shift makes the head feel heavier and increases both the bending moment and torque on the shaft during the swing. (Note that what the golfing industry calls "torque" in a shaft is actually a measure of its torsional stiffness. A shaft has no inherent property of torque; torque is the rotational moment imparted to the shaft when the clubhead—whose center of mass lies outside the shaft—is accelerated. When you read that a shaft has four degrees of torque, this means the tip end of the shaft rotates four degrees relative to the fixed handle end when subjected to a standard amount of torsion.)

Does a graphite shaft offer an improved feel? This is a purely subjective matter. I have heard several friends on the Senior Tour claim that the graphite shaft reduces the amount of shock transmitted back up to the hands when the clubhead strikes the ball, and I'm sure that there's an element of truth to this claim.

When you compare the technical specifications for graphite shafts to those of steel shafts, it's striking that the steel shaft specs do not mention torque. I have read that this is because all steel shafts have a torque rating of around two degrees, but why not list this parameter if it's so important for graphite shafts? My own cynical interpretation of this inconsistency is that the industry makes more money on the higher-priced graphite product. You can surround it with a bunch of marketing baloney and golfers will buy the gimmick. But the only way you can make a graphite shaft that approaches the torsional stiffness of a steel version is to "lace" the graphite with some very expensive boron or titanium—and even then the best torque ratings will be around two and a half degrees, but not two degrees. So the best alloyed graphite shafts have somewhat less torsional resistance than steel. This, coupled with the higher concentration of weight in the clubhead because of the shaft's lighter weight, makes the graphite-shafted club inherently harder to control.

For higher-handicap players and slower swingers, ladies and juniors, the use of a shaft with higher torque rating as well as greater flexiblity appears to be helpful in getting the clubface squared up at impact and helping cure the dreaded slice. At impact with any design of shaft, the driver's clubface will have overtaken the shaft and caused a slight reverse bend in the shaft. Top players want this effect to be negligible, so they play stiffer shafts with a lower torque rating. The less strong players and those who cut across the ball in a pronounced manner (this includes the vast majority of golfers) can benefit from increasing the overtaking at impact, which tends to add loft and close down the clubface.

TIPPING

Most driver shafts are produced in forty-six-inch lengths with a three-and-a-half- to four-inch parallel tip at the bottom. The shaft will be shortened typically to forty-three inches for a men's driver. If the length is taken from the handle end, leaving the long tip intact, the shaft will be more flexible, tend to promote a higher ball flight, and have a softer feel. Stronger players often have a portion of the length reduction taken from the tip to increase stiffness. Shafts are also available with varying degrees of tip stiffness. And some shaft designs feature a tapered tip, which eliminates the possibility of tipping.

BEND AND BALANCE POINT

Shafts are available with high, mid, and low bend points. This variable seems to affect feel and not ball flight. The lower the bend point, the greater the feel that seems to be fed back from the clubhead. The balance point of the shaft refers to its center of mass. The farther down the shaft this point lies, the heavier the club will feel.

The Driver Grip

A grip is the proper size for your hand when the tip of your left-hand forefinger (the right-hand forefinger for southpaws) just barely touches your left-thumb heelpad. Grips can be ordered standard, oversized, or undersized. The variety of materials available is too great to cover here; I suggest you visit www.golfworks.com or get hold of one of their catalogs. Simply reading through this catalog is a great way to expand your knowledge.

Over time grips of any type become slippery due to wear but also due to a buildup of residue from your hands. Periodic scrubbing with Comet can make a worn-out grip seem like new until it's truly worn out. You need to keep grips of excellent condition and proper size on all your golf clubs.

A Selection Guideline Procedure

Armed now with the vocabulary, you're ready to choose a driver. First, visit www.swingweight.com and read through articles reviewing the performance of any driver you are thinking about buying. Second, visit www.golfworks.com or get one of their recent catalogs and look at their offerings in driver heads and shafts. You do not have to spend seven hundred dollars to get armed with the latest driver technology. For about half that price you can have a custom clubmaker build your driver exactly to your specifications.

Next, identify roughly your shaft's desired flexibility, torque, and construction using these guidelines:

DISTANCE YOU FLY YOUR DRIVES

150 yards = most flexible shaft, high torque, graphite
180 yards = slightly less flexible shaft, medium torque
210 yards = regular shaft, medium torque, graphite or steel
240 yards = stiff shaft, low torque, boron-graphite or steel
270+ yards = extra stiff, low torque, boron-graphite or steel

Now determine the best driver length for you by experimenting with different lengths. A good idea is to place a thin strip of marking tape on the face, hit ten drives, and then observe the scatter pattern. Do this with the different lengths you're considering. The best length for you will have the tightest impact pattern on the marking tape. Begin your search using a standard-length men's or ladies driver. It is surprising how often these turn out to be the best. Maybe that's why they have come to be called "standard."

At this point you are very close to identifying the best club for your swing. If you're a slicer and thinking about using a driver with an offset hosel and/or closed face, try to borrow one or pick one up secondhand to make sure you like it. Experiment! Pro shops now routinely stock a wide range of "demo" drivers.

As to metal head material, go with your inclination and pocketbook. There is no solid evidence that one or another of the metals available propels the ball farther given the exact same head design. The more expensive, higher-strength titanium does allow more selective perimeter weighting, with the potential of increased accuracy. If accuracy is not your problem and you fly your present drives 220 yards or more consistently, you may want to consider the spring-face designs. If accuracy is already your main problem, then this is not the solution.

In summary, as you go through the process of selecting a new driver, remember that you are also working to improve the basic elements of your swing to produce long and straight drives and to lower your handicap. If you manage to find a driver that compensates for all your swing faults, no matter how extreme they may be, this driver will tend to lock you into these very faults and work against making you a better golfer.

PART I

Inescapable Fundamentals

A s we start into the fundamentals, here are some ideas on how to implement improvements to your swing.

We learn to successfully hit a golf ball in two distinct ways. First, we learn the static fundamentals of grip, posture, stance, and ball position. These basics are a matter of initial learning and repetition, straightforward and necessary, but very often neglected. Second, after we start the club back, we enter a dynamic world in which we perceive our bodies reacting to gravity and the mass of the club and its impact with the ball. The goal in nearly every full-length shot is to achieve a position prior to impact that ensures a powerful, square blow will be delivered to the golf ball. The advice we are given is often quite vague:

- ➤ Swing through to the target.
- ➤ Retain the wrist cock for the late hit.
- ➤ Extend on the takeaway.
- ➤ The club should be parallel at the top.
- ➤ Hit from the inside out.
- ➤ Don't sway.

In every case the beginning golfer or frustrated veteran could legitimately complain, "Yeah, but how much?" or "How can I tell? I can't see myself."

There are four elements involved in solving this dynamic dilemma:

1. Pick an excellent swing to model yours upon.
2. Physically memorize—using mirror, camera, and instructor—the dynamic positions you hope to achieve, *with the greatest emphasis on the positions just prior to and at impact.*
3. Use drills to ingrain the muscle memory of the correct swing.
4. Commit yourself to constant feedback and continual improvement.

One of the worst bits of advice offered by top players and instructors is to practice swing changes only on the practice tee. This may be a good idea if you have several hours a week to spend on the practice tee, but the vast majority of golfers don't have that luxury. As you read this book and make changes to your golfing technique, take these changes with you. If you need to fix your grip or posture, do it and never look back. It will soon feel natural.

Once you're on the course it *is* important not to have *too* many swing thoughts at the same time. I recommend no more than two swing thoughts on any particular shot. For example, you may want to think about a smooth takeaway and making sure you get your right elbow reconnected to your right hip on the downswing. Or you may want to focus on keeping your right arm and shoulder muscles very relaxed and attempting to achieve the perfect impact position you have memorized. Or you could focus on keeping your weight on the inside of your right foot at the top of the swing and then driving your right knee and hip toward the target to start the downswing. There really is an inexhaustible supply of beneficial swing thoughts, and it's very helpful, when repeated bad shots begin, to change from one pair of swing thoughts to another.

All golfers, even very good golfers, have their own private set of swing problems. Whenever I go too long without checking myself in the mirror or on tape, it is a certainty that when I do check, I'll find that my stance has grown too narrow, my hands are too low at address, and I'm not making a strong enough rotational turn away from the ball with my shoulders. These have always been my tendencies and always will be.

The golfers I have tried to help over the years just do not comprehend the tenaciousness of their own swing fault tendencies. When a pro advises students that they're swaying by rolling their weight to the outside of the right foot at the top of the backswing, a few swings on the lesson tee are usually all that's needed to eliminate the problem, and the pupils will certainly be hitting the ball much better. When the pro sees these players on the first tee a week later, though, 95 percent of the time they will have reverted to the sway. But when you ask them if they still sway, they'll swear to you that they've fixed the problem.

When you set out to change your swing for the better, understand that even though you may make initial progress, without constant visual checking or verification from a good instructor you will slide quickly back to your old ways. Try to accept that you may go through some extended periods of awkwardness before the change begins to feel natural. When the best players in the world find themselves struggling, they always go back to the basics and begin rebuilding. It is a never-ending process of continual improvement based on repeatedly returning to the inescapable fundamentals.

1

The Rules
of Impact

Rule 1: The Momentum Law

For a given clubhead speed, the maximum possible momentum will be transferred to the golf ball when the clubhead is traveling down the intended path of the target and the clubhead is perfectly square to the target during the milliseconds that the ball remains in contact with the clubhead.

As I mentioned in the introduction along with figure 1, the three primary ingredients for obeying Rule 1 are:

1. Right elbow on right hip.
2. Retained wrist cock until just prior to impact.
3. Clubhead on a distinctly inside-out path.

Rule 2: The Law of Approximate Perfection

Various combinations of grip, posture, and swing path can produce very useful approximations of the ideal position at impact.

Whereas Rule 1 appears a bit severe, Rule 2 offers many rays of hope. The sketch in figure 3 shows a representation of the clubhead path and target line as seen from directly above the golfer. The two ellipses illustrate the clubhead path for an upright and flat swing.

Golfers strive for unattainable perfection. Happily, some very different and even some flawed swings can work pretty well. Every shot is a compromise. Hogan is generally recognized as the greatest striker of the ball ever, and he claimed there were rarely more than two or three swings per round with which he was satisfied. Fortunately, even a crude approximation of solid hit appears to provide enough glimpse of the Promised Land that a 20 handicapper can become hooked and tormented for life. The endeavor is so difficult and mystical that human beings, usually prone to cheerfully annihilating one another, gang up against the gods and actually root for other humans.

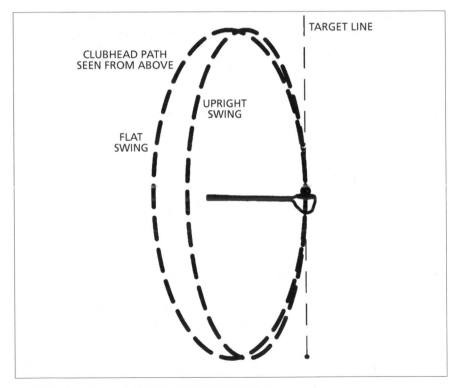

FIGURE 3: FLAT AND UPRIGHT SWING PLANES

In one of my all-too-infrequent appearances on the correct side of the ropes, I was paired with Arnold Palmer in a Senior Tour event. We had a small gallery by his standards—seemed like at lot to me. What surprised me the most was to discover just how hard the folks outside the ropes were rooting for me (or for anyone else who might have been in my predicament that day). I could feel it so strongly that I hit a number of silly shots trying to impress them. None of these silly shots worked, of course, nor did the one in which Arnold actively tried to cheer me on. I had qualified in with an extremely hot putter, which only just barely made up for a very nasty and unpredictable duck hook that would appear several times per round just when I thought it was gone. When we got to the fourteenth tee at Wilshire Country Club, I had gotten back to just 2 over and had had the honors for a few holes. As I stood back to line up my drive on the reachable par 5, Arnold said to me and to the crowd, "Okay, Frank, let's really let one rip here!" Not surprisingly, my drive turned left about 50 yards off the tee, went horizontal like a Frisbee, crossed the rough line at 100 yards, crossed the first row of trees at 125, cleverly threaded its way through another row of trees, then collided with a very attractive live oak and settled into its root structure. Thanks, Arnold!

You don't have to make absolutely perfect contact!

Back to Rule 2, the Law of Approximate Perfection. In figure 4 I have rotated the clubhead path by ten degrees, producing a pronounced "cutting-across" action. This seemingly gross deviation from perfection results in an astonishingly small loss of power because the cosine of 10 degrees is 0.985. In simple English, the power available along the target line has been reduced only by 1.2 percent of its maximum possible value. With a drive that flies 270 yards, this represents a sacrifice of less than 4 yards. If the clubface itself remains square to the target line at impact, a powerful blow will be delivered that starts the ball slightly left with a self-correcting spin, thereby producing a power fade—one of the true wonders of nature. The spin of a power fade tends to keep the ball in the air and make it land softly and stay put.

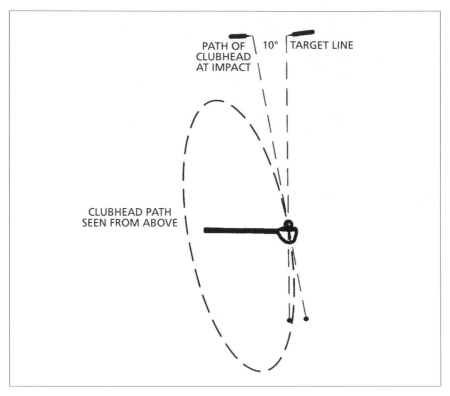

PATH OF \ 10° | TARGET LINE
CLUBHEAD
AT IMPACT \ |

CLUBHEAD PATH
SEEN FROM ABOVE |

FIGURE 4: IMPACT FOR THE POWER FADE

And it works the other way, too. With an inside-out swing path and a square clubhead at impact, a draw spin is imparted to the ball. Even if the angle of contact for a cut or a draw is increased to twenty degrees, the loss of power is still only 6 percent, or 16 yards off a 270-yard ball flight. The vast majority of top-notch players do not try to hit very many straight shots. A grooved swing along either deviation from perfect seems to result in shots of greater predictability. It's a wise economic decision to give up a yard or two and make more frequent appearances on the short grass.

A word of caution is in order about the draw or hook. Because the clubface is slightly de-lofted at impact, the ball generally comes out hotter, lands harder, and rolls farther. A very select few have had the coordination to control this shot really well. Arnold Palmer, Julius Boros, and Jim Colbert come to mind. These individuals are/were blessed with extraordinary coordination, even by tour standards. Their every physical action resembles a choreographed dance step. They cannot help being that graceful. The rest of us more average mortals should approach the hook with caution. It is Sam Snead who is credited with the quote, "You can talk to a fade, but a hook just won't listen."

Rule 3: The Law of the Leading Hands

In every golf shot, the hands must lead the clubhead at impact.

Rule 3 is nonnegotiable. No amount of filibustering can get around it. You can blame your tops, sculls, and wild slices on the devil, a passing car, the wind, or an inconsiderate opponent. The inescapable fact, however, is that you did not lead with your hands. Many golfers acquire the bad habit of letting the clubhead get ahead at impact in the hope of lifting the ball into the air. I agree that it's counterintuitive to consider hitting down on the ball to make it lift up and get airborne, so I can sympathize with the beginner who inevitably falls into this trap.

Hit down to make the ball go up!

My favorite analogy for Rule 3 relates to downhill skiing. In normal conditions, the skier must lean down the hill and weight up the forward part of her skis to gain control of the mountain. To the beginning skier, however, it's counterintuitive and even frightening to lean into a hill when gravity is trying to seriously hurt you. Similarly, the beginning golfer must learn to lead with the hands at impact and trust the loft of the club to get the ball airborne.

The photos in figure 5 show just how much the hands lead the clubhead into the impact zone, with the pitching wedge in frame a and with the driver in frame b.

FIGURE 5A & B: THE LAW OF THE LEADING HANDS

Summary of Chapter 1: The Rules of Impact

1. Optimal power comes from the combined momentums of the arms and wrists delivered to the clubhead along the target line. The key elements for achieving power are keeping your right elbow on or near your right hip and retaining the wrist cock until the impact zone.

2. Surprisingly large angles of deviation of the clubhead path from the target line do not result in major losses of power. Slight deviations can, in fact, be very useful.

3. Your hands must be ahead of the clubhead at the impact position.

2

The Concept of Target

Some are born to sweet delight,
some are born to endless night.

—William Blake

A drive long and straight. Long is not much good without straight. Learn to aim or you will be doomed to "endless night." Average golfers stand on the tee or in the fairway a very long way from the goal. They consult distance cards and markers and toss up grass to judge the wind. Sometimes there are philosophical discussions about the perfect shot with playing companions. It would seem self-evident that, after all this fuss, golfers would pick a target. Nonetheless, if you stop them just as they're about to draw the club back, rudely interrupt, and demand to know exactly what particular line or object they're aiming for, you will likely not get a crisp answer. So I ask myself: *If they aren't aiming at anything precise, how do they hope to arrive precisely on target?*

Advanced golfing swing theory often tries to help golfers who don't know how to hit down on the golf ball and don't bother to aim it. In this chapter you will be taught a very simple means for repetitively picking a target and aligning your swing to that target. You will learn a practice method to reinforce correct alignment. This practice method will surely help you excavate golf balls from good and bad lies alike and send them on their way toward the target!

If I had to guess a percentage, I would say that 90 percent of all golfers never really pick a target. If I had to guess a reason, it would be that the simple process of aligning correctly is just too confusing for folks who've never been shown how simply it can be done. It requires really considering the consequences of a poorly struck shot and making rational choices. I think it makes many golfers even more apprehensive to focus on likely unpleasant outcomes of the shot. Lacking any concept of how to control the ball at impact, these golfers seem to find aiming frightening and irrelevant.

The first step toward repetitive and reliable aiming is to ingrain it into your practice sessions. Figure 6 shows the simple method I use in nearly every practice session. First I find a level spot on the practice tee. I tee up the first ball to be struck, then stand behind the ball and pick out an object that is to be my target. Pointing roughly north is not good enough; you must pick out an exact object. Then I address the ball and lay a 2- or 3-iron on the ground parallel to my toes and offset by three or four inches, as shown in figure 6.

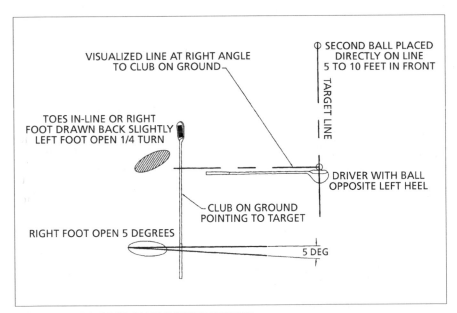

FIGURE 6: PRACTICE ALIGNMENT METHOD

Next, I step back and inspect the alignment of this club to my target and adjust it so that it's dead on. Then I place a second ball aligned with the target about five or ten feet in front of the ball to be struck. In an early book, Jack Nicklaus talked about picking a spot about three feet in front of the ball. In a later book, *The Full Swing*, he refers to finding a spot about ten feet in front of and in line with the target. I find that anything between five and ten feet works well for me. I am going to use this ball to make sure my clubhead is correctly aligned and to square up my shoulders and hips. Three feet is just too close for me to accomplish all this. The potential angle of error is substantially less if the ball is farther out front.

Once I have placed the forward ball, I step back to make sure that it is indeed in line. All this may seem tedious and time consuming, but in actual fact I will have invested only about thirty seconds to get to this point prior to beginning my practice session. The club on the ground serves several very useful purposes. First of all, it reinforces my mental image of a swing path traveling down the target line at impact. Second, I use it to set my feet. Third, I use it to square up my shoulders and hips along the target line. Fourth, by holding the club in my hand perpendicular to the club on the ground, I can quickly check the ball position relative to my feet and make sure that, with the driver, it is played from a point in line with my left heel.

At this point I have no more than one minute invested, and I step back to ensure one final time that the two balls and the club on the ground are in line with my target. So now I'm ready to begin my practice session. I know that on each and every shot, I will be correctly aligned. I'm building and reinforcing good habits, not bad ones. The constant reinforcement of correct alignment will instinctively be carried from the practice tee to the course. It is also advisable, during a round, to check your alignment by occasionally laying a club down along the edges of your toes after lining up to an imaginary target.

The great majority of players do not achieve anything but the random excavation of dirt on the practice tee. On most of my shots from the practice tee, I first stand behind the ball and sight my target—just as if I were on the course—and try to visualize the flight of the shot I'm about to hit. In this way, I am reinforcing with each practice shot a sense of correct alignment, ball positioning, and positive visualization.

Alignment on the Course

Once you're on the course with this physical training ingrained, the alignment and execution of each shot requires some structure and discipline. Nearly every golf instruction book I have seen does a credible job of defining the main elements of "on the course" alignment. These elements are:

1. Standing behind the golf ball, deciding the shot to be played, and picking out a distinct object as a target for alignment.

2. Envisioning the shot exactly as you hope to pull it off.

3. Moving up to the ball and placing the clubhead behind the ball, square to this target line, making sure that your shoulders and hips are parallel to the target line.

4. Setting your feet to complete the correct alignment and ball positioning for the shot at hand.

As a high school player this final aspect of aligning my feet gave me much trouble from time to time. Upon placing a club down along the line of my toes in the completed stance, I would find that I had worked myself into either a very closed or a very open position. During our freshmen year at Michigan, John Schroeder gave me a tip that has forever eliminated this problem. When you place your feet, first position your right foot as close as possible to where it will end up. Then visualize a line from the toe of your right foot to the target and place your left foot in relation to this line. Done in this order, the process will give you much better alignment consistently than if you place your left foot first and then try to position the right. It has been my observation that most average golfers really don't have any discipline or routine for repetitively setting their feet—and those who do, tend to set the left foot first.

This chapter has, I hope conveyed to you the importance of aiming and provided a means to get you aligned with your target. It is nearly impossible to overemphasize the importance of mastering this fundamental element of the game of golf. As you apply these methods initially, you may feel restricted by the routine and sense a loss of naturalness in your golf swing. Stick with it! Correct alignment will become second nature, and soon you'll be able to use your natural rhythm and athletic skills within a correct and repetitive framework.

3

Posture, Rhythm, and Tempo

Striking a golf ball is a left-brained, instinctual, and artistic athletic endeavor. This idea may surprise golfers who see the game as a right-brained activity, a nearly endless set of rules and analytical exercises. These golfers are likely to view the learning process as no more than training the body to execute certain precise moves and memorizing the various address positions best suited for each type of shot. We do indeed have to learn certain fundamentals to enable the possibility of a correctly struck golf ball. Examining the fundamentals, we try to explain logically what happens in a good swing. As we analyze and try to explain, it is very easy for the student to grab the stick by the wrong end and conclude that logic and analysis precede all else. A common result of getting this stick the wrong way around is "paralysis by analysis." All the great golf swings have superimposed marvelous timing and athletic skills onto a rock-solid framework of swing fundamentals.

In golf, the term *rhythm* describes the overall timing of one body part to another, the coordinated and balanced swinging of the hands, arms, and shoulders with the balanced turning of the torso against first the bracing, and ultimately the driving and release of the legs. *Tempo* refers to the sequence of speed and the overall speed at which these coordinated movements occur. Correct posture and grip are the vital ingredients that allow rhythm and tempo to be beautifully applied.

The black solid lines in the sketch in figure 7 show the ideal posture. The dashed lines show the mistake made by the majority of golfers. Even tour players have to constantly guard against slumping into this troublesome position. Frequent checking of the posture in a mirror or, better yet, on videotape seems to be the only way to prevent backsliding into a slumpy address position. The ideal posture promotes good balance by keeping your body's overall center of gravity halfway between your heels and toes. The flex in your knees allows your legs to do their work of bracing solidly against the turn during the backswing and to be driven toward the target on the downswing. Notice the nearly straight line of the back, with the head held high. This allows you to swing the club freely. It promotes a consistent and balanced turn. And most importantly, this posture helps you more easily get your hands behind yourself on the backswing—which in turn allows the clubhead to deliver a square blow to the ball at impact.

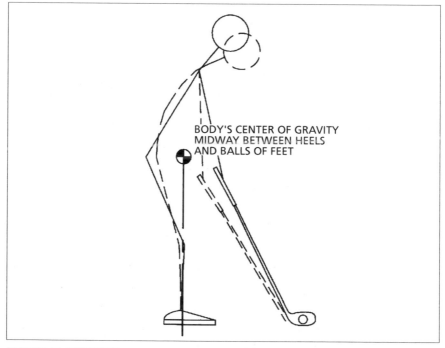

BODY'S CENTER OF GRAVITY MIDWAY BETWEEN HEELS AND BALLS OF FEET

FIGURE 7: POSTURE

The correct posture shown in figure 7 does not initially feel very natural, and it's somewhat difficult to attain repeatedly. A disciplined approach is required until the correct posture becomes your natural position.

Three-Step Method for Achieving Good Posture

1. Starting from a perfectly erect posture, thrust your hips backward and flex your knees, placing the lower half of your body into the position shown in figure 7 while maintaining your spine and head in a straight line, still very much erect. Check yourself in a mirror to ensure that you are getting step 1 correct.

2. Take a correct grip on your club with the shaft of the club held horizontal to the ground.

3. While maintaining the lower-body position of step 1, rotate your upper body about the hip sockets, still keeping all curvature out of your lower spine. Again, check your position in the mirror and compare to the lines of figure 7.

Using a disciplined approach, you can easily learn and maintain good posture. Check yourself regularly in a mirror or window. Use correct posture when you practice and play from now on. It will feel weird for a day or two and from then on begin to feel natural.

Do you have to match the ideal posture to play good golf? No! Consider Jim Furyk, Hubert Green, Miller Barber, or many others who have made a living playing golf with imperfect posture. Does it help to have a posture that approximates the ideal? Yes! Consider Jones, Hogan, Mickey Wright, Woods, Snead, Nicklaus, and Watson, to list just a few of the greatest ball strikers of all time. Is it a coincidence that each of these golfers had nearly perfect posture at address and maintained it throughout the swing?

Try to adopt perfect posture. Even if it's not comfortable for you, there is still plenty of hope. Although both an unorthodox grip and an inelegant posture can and will lead to an unusual-looking swing, at the moment of impact only the clubhead makes contact with the ball.

Avoid Getting Overmechanical

The most beautiful and effective golf swings have always possessed great posture, rhythm, and tempo. These elements are essential for you to arrive at the impact zone in a correct and powerful position. When you see tapes of the great swings or happen to see one in person, don't just look at the mechanics. You should also try to grasp a sense of the rhythm and tempo of this player's golf swing and the preparatory movements just prior to the hit. These seemingly random movements, including the waggle, are analogous to the dribbling, flexing of the knees, and spinning of the basketball in the hands of a good free-throw shooter. Like the foul shooter, the golfer is striving for a sense of rhythm and tempo while at the same time building a positive mental image of a pure swish or a drive curved perfectly to match the dogleg in a fairway. As you read this book or if you are struggling with your game, pull out a tape of Sam Snead's golf swing, study that swing, and try to mimic Sam's rhythm and tempo.

I remember well my first exposure to another of golf's great swings. It was the 1971 Western Amateur, the practice tee at the Point-of-Woods in Benton Harbor, Michigan, late in the day after the second round of qualifying. I was fresh out of the army with a very rusty golf swing and a complete lack of confidence. My strong play in the '67 and '68 NCAAs seemed to belong to another lifetime and person. As I labored away at a pile of balls trying to find a swing that would work, I became aware of the unusually loud and very frequent impact of a driver just behind me. *Whack! Whack! Whack!* Certainly it was only one person creating all this racket, but how could the next ball be teed up and shot struck so quickly and purely as this? A poorly struck golf ball does not sound anything like what I was hearing.

When I turned I discovered a small, freckled redhead with oversized forearms, oblivious to everything else on the planet and apparently intent upon ripping the cover from each ball. Like Hogan, his tempo was quick and the rhythm was pure upper crust, the *crème de la crème.*

Later that summer I would be photographed with Tom Watson when we were first-round leaders of the PGA Tour local qualifier, held at the country club in Quincy, Illinois. Since I had been a junior member there in high school, I knew every blade of grass on the golf course and with the additional help of an outrageously hot putter had managed a 65, one behind Watson's 64.

In those days Tom was even longer than in his major championship years. As I watched him in Michigan in '71, he would get his left wrist a little bit laid off at the top of a fairly steep backswing and then attack the ball with incredible velocity in his arms and a perfectly timed explosive release of his wrists. Later in that practice session I overheard someone ask what he had hit for his second shot on the ninth hole, a 465-yard par 4, slightly uphill if I remember it right. I know I was using a 2- or 3-iron if I had hit a good 260-yard drive. Watson's answer, "A 9-iron," helped me understand that I should go to work as an engineer.

Good posture, rhythm, and tempo are needed to arrive repeatedly at a functional impact position with enough clubhead velocity to produce

1971 Tour School Local Qualifying: FIRST-ROUND LEADERS, TOM WATSON, 64, AND GROVES, 65

something like the desired shot. Golfers such as Snead, Watson, Couples, Boros, Geiberger, Littler, and Els come to mind as examples to copy. The conventional guidelines of swing theory (proper grip, posture, and stance) can obviously be interpreted with some poetic license if you will learn to swing down and through the ball with as much rhythm and tempo as you can muster. The lists etched on the traveling trophies of the major championships are littered with names of players with un-conventional swings, but not a single name appears belonging to a player without good rhythm and tempo and a decent posture.

Golf has a mystery that inspires metaphysical analogies. Proper fundamentals of grip and posture are the yang, and rhythm and tempo the yin. Golf is athletic artistry and creativity superimposed upon an under-lying set of fundamentals. It is a holistic mind-and-body experience. The right brain must provide structure and make rational decisions without impairing the left-brained execution of the deed itself. Later, as we move on to the practical task of crushing a driver long and straight, never forget to try to stand correctly and make each swing with good rhythm and tempo.

4

Gripping the Club for Power at Impact

A proper grip on the club is undeniably a basic requirement for building a good golf swing. Your brain and the rest of your body can only communicate with golf club via your hands. Any serious golfer who ever saw Sam Snead or Arnold Palmer taking a grip has appreciated the artistry and beauty involved. Hands by Michelangelo with incredible strength melded into a working unit equally capable of the most delicate finesse.

Every golf book written since Prohibition has advocated nearly the same method of holding the club. Although the list of top-notch golfers with strange grips is sizable, the vast majority of players since then have adhered more or less precisely to Harry Vardon's method of holding the club. It is a curious fact that both Nicklaus and Woods have deviated from the conventional wisdom by using the interlocking grip that is normally recommended for players with small hands. Any of the many golf instruction books will direct you along the path to a good grip. I have never seen a one that recommends a seriously improper grip. My own favorite is Hogan's description of the grip in his *Five Lessons: The Modern Fundamentals of Golf.* I strongly recommend that you use Hogan's book and follow Ben's instructions almost to a T.

As you look at the photos of my grip in this chapter, you will notice that both the right and the left hands are in slightly stronger positions than those recommended in Hogan's book. Hogan was describing what he did in his mature years as the undisputed greatest ball striker who ever lived. As he learned the game, he did so with a significantly stronger grip; he later made subtle modifications in his search for perfection. *I believe the process of learning the game and learning to deliver a square blow to the golf ball is initially aided by a stronger grip.* As a youngster I played with a much stronger grip; my left hand in particular was strong, and it helped me make solid contact and produce a hook that would run a very long way on unwatered fairways.

A pro golfer grips a golf club two to three hundred times a day and pays, each and every time, a great deal of attention to this seemingly simple gesture. As soon as the hands are in place on the club, the waggling begins. Waggling provides a means of testing the feel of the grip, associating that particular grip with the correct hinging of the wrists, and reinforcing muscle memory for the upcoming impact with the ball. The ideal grip allows your wrists to cock and unleash with great freedom and power (in fact, freedom equals power) along the correct path as your arms swing down this same path. If you get the grip wrong, you will force your body into strange contortions trying to make solid contact with the

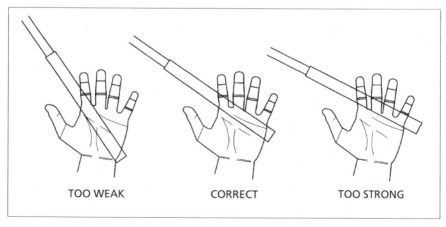

TOO WEAK   CORRECT   TOO STRONG

FIGURE 8: LEFT-HAND GRIP

ball. Find a golfer with an unusual swing and you will almost always find a strange grip!

For the left-hand grip, position the club as shown in the center view of figure 8 and wrap your hand around the club. When standing in the impact position with this grip on the club, the V made by your thumb and forefinger should point directly toward your right shoulder. You should see only one or one and a half knuckles of the four fingers of your left hand in the impact position. If you return to the address position, then two and a half to three knuckles will be visible and the V should point to your right shoulder. The "pressure" fingers of your left hand are the last three: middle, ring finger, and pinkie. They effectively trap the club against the heel of your left palm.

The photos in figure 9 show this "trapping" action in frame a. In frame b, I have simply wrapped my last three fingers on the club shaft then removed my thumb and forefinger to illustrate the "pressure" fingers of the left-hand grip.

Keep Your Right-Hand Grip in the Fingers

For the right hand, position your open hand onto the club so that your palm is parallel to the clubface and both your palm and the clubface are

FIGURE 9A & B: TRAPPING THE CLUB WITH THE LEFT-HAND GRIP

square to the target. In Nick Faldo's book *Golf—The Winning Formula,* he describes the right-hand grip as similar to the way you'd hold a tennis racket for a forehand shot. This is a very useful analogy to help understand the grip of the right hand. There are really no pressure fingers in the right hand that are as active as the last three fingers of your left hand. The amount of squeeze in your right-hand fingers is comparable to that involved in throwing a baseball. Try throwing a baseball with a very tight grip on the ball. You will lose both velocity and control. Figure 10 is a sketch showing the proper positioning of the club in the right hand; the

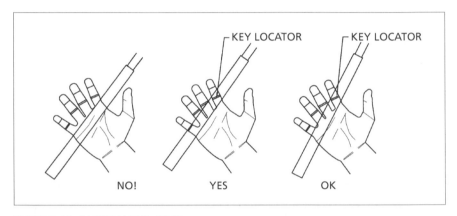

FIGURE 10: RIGHT-HAND GRIP

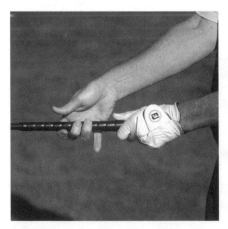

FIGURE 11: RIGHT-HAND GRIP IN THE FINGERS

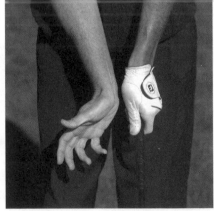

FIGURE 12: GRIP AND WRIST COCK

photo in figure 11 illustrates how the club is cradled in the fingers of my right hand. The club is held very much more in the fingers of the right hand than most golfers seem to realize.

The photo in figure 12 shows my left hand already in proper position on the club and my right hand about to complete the grip. My right hand is hinged backward to illustrate the proper wrist cock. Note that the palm of my right hand faces directly at the target.

Figure 13 shows the desired hinging of both hands and wrists as they are taken away at the start of the swing and as they approach impact. My right hand is left just off the grip to better illustrate the action. Note how much my left forearm in figure 13 has rotated when compared to figure 12. The final motions just before impact are the release of this stored left-forearm torsion and the release of your right-hand hinge. (Note that I did not say *casting* of your right hand. In this last move before impact, your right hand returns to the address position, and it stays there until well past impact.)

These two correctly timed releases of stored power used in conjunction with the arm speed generated by the proper coiling and uncoiling of your upper torso result in a great acceleration of clubhead speed at impact. Figure 14 shows my completed grip. My hands are closely melded into a single, relaxed unit allowing maximum freedom of wrist action.

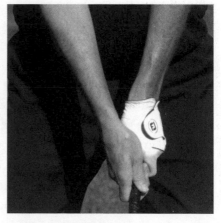

FIGURE 13: CORRECT HINGING
ACTION OF WRISTS

FIGURE 14: COMPLETED GRIP

Note the orientation of my elbows. My right elbow points to my right hip, thus allowing my right arm to fold naturally into my right side as the backswing progresses. My left elbow points about halfway between my left hip and the target. Many golfers make their mistake of letting the elbows point outward, or allowing the insides of the elbows to point at each other. This results in a flying "chicken wing" of a right arm and makes it nearly impossible to keep the left arm straight.

All bad grips seem to have two things in common: The hands are placed in such a way that the wrists cannot function freely, and the grip is too tight.

Avoid Regripping during the Swing

It is also possible to place your hands on the club correctly and then destroy this good work by changing your grip during the swing (regripping) or incorrectly maintaining the correct pressure points within the grip. All my mid- to high-handicap friends regrip the club either during their waggle or very soon after the swing begins.

Once again we return to Ben Hogan's book to find the correct means to combat these tendencies. In his section on the grip and on the jacket of Hogan's book you will find a sketch of Ben swinging with the thumb and forefinger of his right hand removed from the shaft. This simple drill combats the tendencies both to regrip and to lose the correct pressure point during the swing. Use this check repeatedly as you learn the drills in the following chapters.

Through the years I've worked with many golfers to try to improve their grips. Sadly, my success ratio is not greater than about 50 percent. Those who've failed to change their grips have done so by paying insufficient attention to a seemingly obvious detail. Although they've learned all about the Vs pointing to the right shoulder and many other nuances of a good grip, they forget that the grip must be taken with the clubhead set *square* to the target line. It does no good to grip the club as perfectly as Sam Snead did if the clubface is fifteen degrees shut. The idea is to get your hands and the club to work together!

As you learn to grip the club correctly, keep a club handy around the house for rehearsing. Check the position of the two Vs. Check in the mirror to see that your hands are in the position shown in figure 14 and that the clubface is squared up to the target line. Practice waggling and swinging the club with the correct grip while maintaining a very light hold on the club, primarily with pressure on the last three fingers of your left hand as they trap the club into the heel of your left palm. Use a correct grip from now on whenever you play or practice and spend a few minutes rehearsing each day at home. Within a couple of weeks your old, bad grip will feel just as strange to you as the correct grip did when you first adopted it.

PART II

The Essence of Power

The worst golfers visualize their golf swings as a forced manipulation of the clubhead with their arms and give little or no thought to the motions of their legs and torso.

The best golfers swing from the feet up. Primary emphasis is on making correct, repetitive, "big-body" motions with knees, hips, torso, and shoulders. These core elements are the central engine of the golf swing, producing power and control. Your arms, hands, and club are appendages attached to this central engine of power. Standard golf instruction places far too much emphasis on these appendages while neglecting the central engine.

This section explains the workings of these core elements first before taking on the entire coordinated driver swing. Chapters 5 through 9 describe how to correctly get power stored at the top of your backswing, and chapters 10 through 12 offer advice on how to release, control, and maximize that power on your downswing and follow-through.

Power golf is built on a pyramid of fundamentals. At the base of the pyramid are the most essential ingredients of grip, posture, stance, rhythm, and tempo. In the middle section of the pyramid are the core elements of the big-body motions, the powerful and balanced turning of the torso. At the top lie the final touches, the nuances of extracting the last bit of power from your swing potential. This last and least essential set of issues at the tip of the pyramid includes topics such as getting to parallel at the top and the exact position of your wrists at the top. Despite the vast and immediately obvious differences of clubhead and wrist position at the top of the swings of the best touring pros, these topics seem to mesmerize the golf instruction community.

As you strive to develop a power golf swing, have patience! Build a solid base for your golf swing by first mastering the lower levels of the pyramid. Only then will you have harnessed the potential to hit it really long.

5

The Work of the Turn

E very golf shot powerfully struck requires that the clubhead approach the ball on an inside path, square up just prior to impact, and remain squared up until the ball has left the clubface. Unless you make a shoulder turn full enough that your left arm, left hand, and clubhead go around behind your body, you'll slice. There is work involved in making a correct turn. Muscles are stretched and stressed, storing the potential energy that will power the shot. For many years I have recognized the three most common swing faults—broken left arm, swaying and moving the head, and rolling the weight to the outside of the right foot—as "work avoidance." It is no coincidence that 90 percent of all golfers slice the ball rather than hook it. Hooking takes more work than slicing.

It's very important to understand that the shoulder turn is as vital to chip and pitch shots as it is to the drive. A sufficient shoulder turn is a key ingredient in the recipe for long, accurate, and powerful ball striking. Figure 15 shows the correlation between the distance that the left arm swings back and the amount of shoulder turn. In these frames, I have drawn a line between my shoulders and another line down my left arm. The pent-up power of my turn is most apparent in frame c, but my shoulder turn is equally important to the shot lengths shown in frames a and b because it enables the clubhead to approach the ball from an inside path just prior to impact. The angle between the shoulder line and the left arm line at the top diminishes a little as the swing lengthens.

The "one-piece takeaway," another of golf's most common mantras, results from maintaining this angle intact as the swing begins. Viewed from this face-on perspective, at the top of the backswing (figure 15c), my left arm swings progressively more into line with my shoulder line as the swing lengthens. In a drive, the left-arm line will often match the shoulder line, offering further proof that the left arm and the shoulders turn on different planes. Otherwise they would collide.

Figure 16 shows the one-piece takeaway, left hand only, with the driver. My shoulders, rotating about my spine, appear to be dragging my left arm along for the ride. It's very helpful to practice this motion with your left arm only. Without your right hand on the club, your shoulder turn is unrestricted and, therefore, the correct shoulder turn is much more readily sensed and ingrained. Then, when you place your right hand on the club, the muscle memory from the left-hand swing will help you make a complete shoulder turn.

FIGURE 15: GROWTH OF THE TURN

a: top of swing, thirty yards   b: top of swing, fifty to sixty yards

Nearly all of golf's greatest players have made early and strong shoulder turns to begin their swings. Those who haven't, like Trevino and Couples, have made rather drastic correcting moves near the top of the backswing to get the club around behind them enough to deliver a solid blow at impact.

I had my first look at two of the greatest, Hogan and Snead, when they played an exhibition in Quincy, Illinois, in the mid-1950s. Earlier that summer I had played an exhibition in Keokuk, Iowa, with two famous lady golfers—Louise Suggs and Marlene Hagg, as I remember it. So when I heard that Hogan and Snead were coming for an exhibition at Quincy Country Club, I mistakenly assumed with the accumulated wisdom of eleven years that I would be asked to play. Disappointed at not being invited, I was still thrilled to get a firsthand view of these great golfers.

What I noticed most were both the subtle differences between these two wonderful swings, and a number of elements common to Hogan and Snead that I had never observed in even the best of our local golfers.

c: top of swing, 90 yards

FIGURE 16: START OF THE ONE-PIECE TAKEAWAY

First, each of their grips was perfect, and each man took obvious pride and pleasure in getting the club just right in his hands. The elegance of these grips struck me as some sort of secret handshake allowing entrance into an elite club.

Second was the perfect rhythm and timing of each swing, although Hogan's tempo was quicker.

Finally, I noticed that the body, rather than the hands and arms, seemed to be in charge of the swing—and this was most apparent at the takeaway. There was no jerkiness or snatching of the hands, just a wonderfully smooth and gradual acceleration of the pendulum formed by the left arm and club as the head remained perfectly still.

The gracefulness of great swings cloaks the underlying expenditure of energy needed to propel the golf ball great distances with unfailing accuracy—but make no mistake, there is hard work being done, *the work of the turn.*

6

The Torso
Drill

A t the heart of the golf swing lies the body turn. Let's strip away the
stuff about swing planes, grips with long or short thumbs,
supinated left wrist, and the rest of the details common to discussions of
the behavior of the arms and hands. The kinematics of the legs, torso,
shoulders, and head aren't very complex, but they do require some flexibility and balance. If you were to take sequential photos of every Hall of
Fame golfer and strip away the club and the arms from the images, a surprising similarity would appear in some very diverse-looking swings.
The physics of good ball striking demands this core similarity, and the
torso drill will teach the motions to you.

I start in the address position (figures 17a and 17b) of the drive with
my arms folded against my chest, good posture, weight in balance, with
60 percent on my left foot, 40 percent on my right. My weight is evenly
split between the balls of my feet and the heels. The doughnut shows the
approximate center of gravity of my body.

Just prior to initiating the turn, I focus very briefly on the position of
my right hip and right shoulder. During the backswing portion of this
drill, I want absolutely *no* lateral motion of my right hip or right shoulder.
The great majority of right-handed golfers sway as they begin the swing,
allowing the head and the spine to move to the right away from the target.

In photos 17c and 17d I have added lines between my right ankle,
hip, and shoulder. In 17c the dotted line represents the position of these

FIGURE 17: THE TORSO DRILL

a: address position

b: address position

c: initiating the turnaway

d: frontal view

e: top of the backswing

f: frontal view

g: halfway into the downswing

h: frontal view

FIGURE 17: THE TORSO DRILL (CONTINUED)

i: impact

j: finish

k

elements at address, and the solid line connects my ankle, knee, and shoulder in this position midway into the backswing. In 17d there is only one line showing because, from this viewpoint, there has been essentially no change. In 17c it is clear that I have rotated my right shoulder, hip, and—to a much lesser degree—right knee, around behind me. This is what instructors are referring to when they tell you to make your turn "in a barrel."

Note that my right knee does not straighten but remains athletically flexed. Also note in 17d that the line between my knee and hip angles toward the target, just as it did at address. Instructors commonly tell their pupils to avoid swaying by keeping their weight on the inside of their right foot at the top of the backswing. A helpful training device is to place a golf ball under the outside of your right foot. If you learn to turn in a barrel, eliminating lateral motion of your right knee, hip, and shoulder, then your weight physically cannot get to the outside of the right foot.

Make Your Turn around a Steady Spine

The turn initiation I am advocating here is somewhat old-fashioned and at odds with modern theory, which teaches that the legs and hips are to be firmly braced to resist the shoulder turn. This same modern swing theory strongly advocates the one-piece takeaway. The way the human body is put together, these two centerpieces of modern swing theory are mutually exclusive. By not allowing your right hip and knee some initial movement as shown in 17c, your swing is forced into a very upright plane, swaying is much more likely, and your weight transfer is greatly complicated, making the dreaded reverse pivot more likely.

As you practice this drill, your head should remain fairly steady and level. Some lateral head motion is present in nearly all good golf swings. While it's generally helpful to minimize the amount of lateral movement, consider what Bobby Jones wrote: "I think that in putting, as in making every other golf shot, the player ought to forget about his head. Think with it, but not of it."[3]

---

[3] *Bobby Jones on Golf,* "Keeping Head Still—Fallacious Golf Maxim"

As I make this turn away from the ball, the balance of my weight is pulled to the inside of my right foot. This weight shift occurs as a result of my upper-body action, not because I'm doing anything with my legs to force it. Remember to *keep your right shoulder on a turning plane that is perpendicular to your spine* and this will happen naturally.

The photos in 17e and 17f show the position at the top of the back-swing for the torso drill. Note again that in the frontal view, the angles between my right ankle, knee, and hip have not changed from the previous view. The other key elements are the full shoulder turn ninety degrees, with back to target. My body weight is primarily (perhaps 90 percent) on the inside of my right foot. The 10 percent or so of my weight that remains on my left foot is on the inside of the ball of this foot. I could almost lift my left leg and not fall over. My left heel may be ever so slightly off the ground. If I stay in this same posture and crank my shoulders around another ten degrees, then my left heel will lift farther off the ground and my left knee will be pulled farther toward my right knee.

In photo 17e I have again indicated the relative changes in position of my right knee, hip, and shoulder versus 17c. After the initial movement of my right knee slightly backward as shown in 17c, it stays put. After the position shown in 17c and 17d, my right knee becomes a brace against which my upper torso is coiled. The continued turning of my shoulders drags my right hip somewhat farther behind me. At the top of the turn, a line through my hips has rotated thirty to forty degrees from the address position, while a similar line through my knees would show a rotation of fifteen to twenty degrees.

The marker in photo 17f indicates the approximate center of gravity of my body. According to this locator, you wouldn't think that 90 percent of my weight is on my right foot. The confusing factor is that the top of the backswing is a *dynamic* position. Not only are my feet holding my body's gravitational weight, but my right foot is also providing the deceleration force needed to stop the coiling action of my upper torso. By not understanding the dynamics of this position, some of the most prominent instructors unwittingly teach pupils to sway. This most commonly occurs as damaging advice that the backswing turn should be centered over the right leg. Proper coiling takes place about the spine, and when the shoulders are rotated on a plane perpendicular to the spine, the weight shift occurs naturally without any forcing action from the feet or legs.

A great deal of the confusion and many of the contradictions of modern golf swing theory arise from the mistaken conclusion that the greatest golfers of the modern era must necessarily have had the soundest swing principles. Championship golf requires a repetitive swing and a predictable ball flight, but even more it requires sound nerves, focus, supreme determination, and a very good putter. Until the arrival of Tiger Woods, Jack Nicklaus personified the key elements of a champion.

The greatest golf champions, Jones, Hogan, Snead, and Nicklaus, have all produced a significant number of instructional books of outstanding quality and clarity. Each of these players has shown sympathy for the struggles of fellow golfers and has tried to the best of his abilities to help. Jones and Snead played the entirety of their professional careers using essentially the same swing. This is not to say they didn't make constant small changes, ever searching for a swing closer to perfection, or that they didn't continue to acquire a better and better understanding of their own mechanics. On the other hand, Hogan and Nicklaus both made very significant, fundamental swing changes right in the middle of their professional careers. And in each case the change involved moving to a flatter swing plane and a shorter backswing.

Even the Greatest Golf Swings Have Problems

Of these great champions, none worked harder than Jack Nicklaus to promote a general understanding of the principles of his golf swing. Unfortunately, a number of Jack's early swing idiosyncrasies were seized upon and promoted by the golf community as vital ingredients of the swing. Many golfers, myself included, attempted to take the club away square, without letting it fan open as it naturally wants to. When you combine this element with a more upright swing striving for great extension, you get a steep swing that will tend either to sway or to reverse pivot unless your legs are very active to force a proper hip turn. The underlying complexity of Jack's swing caused some extended periods of very poor play by his standards. As he matured, he found it necessary to revamp his swing to a flatter swing plane for his left arm and a flatter turning plane for his shoulders. With these improvements it became much easier for him to get the clubhead around behind into proper hitting position with less of a flying right elbow and less of a forced hip turn. We can only speculate how many majors Jack would have won had he arrived on tour with the nearly perfect swing of his later years.

In photos 17g and 17h, the downswing begins and several motions take place simultaneously:

➤ My left heel replants firmly (it should have lifted very little, if at all).

➤ My left knee moves toward the target.

➤ My hips move toward the target as uncoiling begins.

➤ My left shoulder moves toward the target.

➤ My right shoulder and elbow drop down.

➤ My right knee and hip drive toward the target.

In frame 17h I have shown with dotted lines the locations of my left knee and hip at the top of the backswing. The solid lines help emphasize the change that has taken place. Because so much is happening at once as the downswing begins, professionals have made numerous efforts to simplify the instructions. Unfortunately, all of the above are needed for a correct transition to the downswing. Telling high handicappers that all they have to do is replant the left foot and spin the hips would be like telling me that the secret to a back flip is to turn my back to the water, lift my arms, and jump. What would follow would not be a pretty sight.

While the motion is complex, it is not particularly difficult to learn by using this drill. Memorize the positions of these photos and then practice in front of the mirror. Work on balance and timing as well as achieving the correct position. *Learning this core movement of the golf swing will be far more helpful than fretting about the position of your hands and arms during the backswing.* Current golf instructional practice completely misses the boat by not emphasizing these common, core motions that lie at the heart of all good swings.

Frame 17i shows the just-beyond-impact position. My weight is almost entirely on my left foot. My left hip has cleared, my right shoulder is low, and my shoulders lie on a plane parallel to the target. My left leg doesn't snap to a straight position until well after impact. Frame 17j shows the finish. My hips and right knee are facing the target. Nearly all my weight is on my left foot.

The work of the turn is most clearly shown in frames 17e and 17f. The work done during a correct backswing results in stored potential energy. This energy takes two forms: first, the coil of your torso anchored by the bracing of your legs, and second, the lifting of your club and arms. The great majority of players manage the lift but leave out the hard part, the coil. For this reason, nearly all bad golf swings can be interpreted as work avoidance.

The most common ways that golfers avoid the work involved in achieving the coiled tension at the top of the backswing are:

➤ Breaking the left arm.
➤ Rolling the weight to the outside of the right foot or swaying.
➤ Picking the club straight up and dropping it down with no real turn.
➤ A seemingly endless number of variations on all of the above, often quite humorous.

It's very helpful to stand in front of a mirror with the correct posture and practice the movements shown in figure 17. In effect, you are learning the primary and inescapable elements of a good full-length golf swing first. By repetitively executing the torso drill with as much tempo and rhythm as possible, you are ingraining a sense of the core elements of the power golf swing. Then you'll have the tools to successfully tackle the more difficult facets of the full swing.

Work on balance as you execute this drill, being sure to keep your center of gravity well centered between your feet. In the frontal-view photos in figure 17, I have shown the location of the approximate center of gravity in this plane. And in figure 17b, I have shown the location in the other plane. Note in frame 17b that a vertical line drawn from this center of gravity to the ground will fall halfway between the heels and balls of my feet. Because my body's center of gravity is always captured between my feet and positioned halfway between my heels and the balls of my feet, my swing will be in balance.

Leg Drive: An Essential Ingredient of Power

Frames 17f and 17h, repeated here, illustrate that simultaneous with my left hip beginning to clear, there must be a lower-body weight shift that transfers a great deal of my body's weight to my left heel. Many top-level golfers have a sense of driving the right hip and right knee toward the target to facilitate this transition. In frame 17f about 90 percent of my weight is on my right foot. In frame 17h only about 40 percent is on my right foot; the other 60 percent has been transferred to my left heel. When you execute this "torso" drill, it should feel like a balanced and rhythmical dance step.

f: frontal view   h: frontal view

Frames 17e and 17g, repeated here, illustrate an important part of this drill. As my left hip begins to clear and my weight is transferred to my left heel, my right hip and right knee, driving forward, retain nearly the same position in these two views. If you leave too much weight on your right foot as your left hip begins to clear, then your right hip and right knee will be forced outward toward the ball. This part of the golf swing certainly demands the most physical coordination and causes trouble, even for the best players in the world. In the real swing, at the same time that your torso moves from position 17e to 17g, your left arm is pulling the club down, your right elbow is being reconnected to your right side, and a great deal of clubhead speed is being created. The greater the length of your backswing, the more patient you must be with your legs and hips at this stage of the swing.

The famous "Snead squat" occurred as Sam began to clear his left hip and knee, went bowlegged in the process as his weight shifted to his left heel, and then held this position as his greatly lifted arms at the top of his

e: top of the backswing   **g:** halfway into the downswing

backswing were reconnected to his body. Sam Snead was almost universally acknowledged as the most graceful man ever to play the game, and the Snead squat was unique to his swing. Given that this peculiarity never appeared in any of the other legends of the game, it should not be recommended to mere mortals. For example, Hogan had absolutely no trace of the bowlegged squat as he entered the downswing, and, rather than separating his knees as his left hip began to clear, he drove both knees and his right hip forward toward the target to shift his weight to his left heel.

Another detail to be learned is that at the just-beyond-impact-position, as shown in frame 17i, my left leg is still flexed. If you spin your hips too soon—before the weight has a chance to transfer to your left heel—then your left leg will snap straight prior to reaching impact. When this happens and the hips are prematurely "spun out," the clubface will close sooner after impact. It is not necessarily fatal given that Tiger Woods demolished the '97 Masters field doing just that, overcoming this defect with tremendous coordination. It appears to me that he has since modified his swing to nearly eliminate this potential problem.

A lot of good players get spun out with their longer clubs and overcome this defect with hand miracles to keep the clubhead square through impact. As long as you're learning this drill, however, you might as well do it as perfectly as possible.

Frame 17j shows the position at the finish of the swing. All my weight is on my left foot, and my hips and shoulders are facing the target. I have clearly "gotten over to the left side" in this photo, and, as a result, there is no trace of the reverse-C shape of the spine that occurs when some weight falls back onto the right foot at the finish.

Figure 17k is the top of the backswing, this time with a line representing the spine, another line showing the perpendicular plane of shoulder rotation, and a third, dotted line representing the swing plane as defined by Hogan. A common problem for golfers is a tendency to turn the shoulders on too steep of a plane. Note the position of my right shoulder in figure 17k—it lies well below the dotted line of my swing plane. (If you are not familiar with the swing plane concept, see figures

21 and 22 and the discussion of these figures in the next chapter.) Many golfers have too much lifting of the right shoulder at the top of the back-swing. When the right shoulder is lifted up from the line shown perpendicular to my spine, it causes the left shoulder to dip down.

When your shoulders are correctly rotated in a plane lying perpendicular to your spine, the weight shift to your right foot during the back-swing becomes a natural event requiring very little conscious effort. If you incorrectly rotate your shoulders on a steeper plane, as I did for thirty years, you will set off a series of inevitable struggles with the reverse pivot, the spun-out impact position, and the reverse-C finish. Great athletes like Johnny Miller and Scott Hoch have gotten rich living with these swing problems, but the average player would do well not to take these troublesome passengers on board.

As you master the torso drill, learn to recognize the torso movements of good players when you see them on the tube or in person. This can be done by forgetting about club, hand, and arm movements and focusing on the body. This will help you recognize the elements that are similar and essential in every good modern golf swing.

7

The Takeaway

Is there only one *truly* correct position at impact? Definitely!

Can very good golf shots result from minor deviations from the perfect impact position? Very definitely.

Is there only one truly correct way to start the golf swing? *Definitely not!*

There are simple, uncomplicated, and aesthetically pleasing ways to initiate the swing and get to the top of the backswing. These can work very well. And there are complicated and unusual ways that work equally well for some unusually talented athletes. Experienced golf instructors come to realize the underlying difficulty of conveying the essentials of solid ball striking to frustrated veterans and beginners. Like Sisyphus with his stone, instructors are bound together with students who metaphorically seem to roll back to the bottom of the hill every time we have pushed them near the top or at least partway up. The only possible hope is to convey simple concepts in small doses.

The takeaway and backswing suggestions contained here are as simple and uncomplicated as I know how to make them. You should ignore them completely if your own method gets you to the top and:

> ➤ You are in balance.
> ➤ Your head has not grossly moved.
> ➤ Your weight is nearly all on the inside of your right foot.
> ➤ You have not rolled out your right knee.

> ➤ You have made a full, powerful shoulder turn.
> ➤ Your weight is not on the toes of your feet.
> ➤ Your foot weight is balanced between your heels and the balls of your feet.
> ➤ Your left arm is straight or nearly so, and your hands are close to being on plane.

For the remaining 99.5 percent of the golfing population, here is a set of simple instructions for arriving at the top of the backswing in an aesthetically pleasing manner consistent with all the items on this list.

Practice the Takeaway with Your Left Arm Only

Figure 18 shows a left-hand-only version of the takeaway with the driver. The true structure of the move is more clearly revealed and the motion is much easier to execute using only your left hand and arm. The vertical line in this figure represents my spine. The top end of the spine line is, of course, closer to the viewer than the bottom of the line because of my address posture.

FIGURE 18: THE ONE-PIECE TAKEAWAY

To initiate the takeaway, I simply rotate my right shoulder and right hip about my spine axis. Keeping my head and the spine axis perfectly in place, the angle between the line through my shoulders and a line along my left arm does not change. Neither my right shoulder nor my right hip has any movement to my right whatsoever. They immediately start going behind me, and my left shoulder starts to move on a path that will lead under my chin.

Another tenet of modern swing theory is that the right knee stays perfectly still as the takeaway occurs. Careful observation of the swings of the great players shows that this isn't true. While the right knee doesn't move much as it resists the turning of the hips and shoulders, it definitely is dragged backward a slight amount. This flexibility greatly facilitates the ease of the takeaway.

This right-knee motion during takeaway is a very subtle issue. As an instructor, I constantly fight the average player's work avoidance tendencies. Swaying the right knee away from the target and rolling the weight to the outside of the right foot are two of the most common methods of work avoidance. So I teach that the right knee must stay in its address position all the way to the top of the backswing. While this is true as seen face-on from the golfer, the photos in figure 19 (repeated from the torso drill) show this subtle movement of the right knee as the swing begins.

The dashed lines in the photo on the right illustrate this change in knee position. As the takeaway begins, my right shoulder, hip, and knee all move backward. Very soon into the backswing my right knee braces

FIGURE 19: BEHAVIOR OF THE RIGHT KNEE AT TAKEAWAY

a: address position   b: just after takeaway

and does not move any farther. My hips continue to turn a bit longer as my right hip is dragged backward by the powerful turning of my shoulders, working against my braced right knee.

If you attempt this move while holding your legs and hips rigid, your shoulders will be forced to rotate on a steeper plane. This steepness takes the club outside the line and invites a number of problems. The players on tour who have the athleticism to overcome a rigid lower body on the takeaway are forced to either live with a fade or to reroute the club at the top so they can deliver a square blow at impact.

Extension Should Be Natural and not Forced

Extension is a buzzword associated with power. Many golfers appear to interpret extension as some sort of reaching action that leads them to lateral head movement, swaying, and loss of balance and power. In figure 18 I clearly have what the golfing world calls "good extension on the takeaway." This is an essential part of a powerful golf swing, but I would define it as an absence of collapse rather than as extension. When I initiate the swing with a one-piece takeaway energized by a strong shoulder turn, extension is an unavoidable by-product.

Figure 20 shows the takeaway, left arm only, slightly farther up the backswing. The lines show that the angle between my shoulders and left arm still haven't changed much from the address angle. It's really the motion of my right shoulder and hip that is powering the takeaway. My left arm is being dragged along for the ride. My left thumb now points away from the target.

FIGURE 20: THE ONE-PIECE TAKEAWAY, CONTINUED

FIGURE 21: THE SWING PLANE

Figure 21 illustrates how the swing plane concept, introduced by Hogan, is useful as a means to determine a very good position for the *hands* at the *top* of the backswing. The line identifying this swing plane runs from the ball up through the tips of my shoulders. In the address position, my hands fall well below this plane. Because Hogan was very short and held his hands very high at address, his left arm was very nearly on plane in the address position. This led to a great deal of confusion for many golfers—myself included—who attempted to be on plane with their left arms and hands throughout the backswing.

If you're of normal stature, your hands will fall more or less below the swing plane at address. The taller you are, the more your hands will tend to be below the line I have drawn. As the takeaway progresses to where your hands are about hip high, your left arm will be much more nearly on this plane.

Understand the Concept of Swing Plane Correctly

The concept of the swing plane, while useful, is perhaps the most abused of all of golf's theories. As first described by Hogan, it's an imaginary sheet of glass whose bottom edge rests on the ground along the target line. It is angled toward you so that the sheet of glass is supported on your shoulders at address.

The figure 22 photos rigorously apply the swing plane concept to my backswing. At address, it is clear that nothing other than my shoulders is on plane. The plane is often interpreted as a guideline for the path that

FIGURE 22: "ON PLANE," DEFINED

a

b

c

d

the clubhead and left arm follow during the backswing. TV commentators can be heard analyzing a pro's swing and saying that all through the backswing he is "on plane." This is an often cheerfully accepted piece of nonsense. In reality, the plane is only relevant at the top of the backswing, where it defines a nearly ideal—but certainly not absolutely required— position for hands and the shaft and face of the club.

In the sequential photos it is apparent that my hands, starting well below the plane at address, progressively close the gap with the swing plane as my backswing gets nearer the top. This is a very individualistic part of the swing. Bobby Jones and the young Sam Snead, for instance, made such a pronounced early shoulder turn that their hands were much more inside the plane line in the position shown in frame c. In the latter stages of the backswing, their hands moved in a nearly vertical manner to reach a perfect, on-plane position at the top.

e

f: "on plane" at the top of the backswing

FIGURE 23: TAKEAWAY COMPARED TO TORSO DRILL POSITIONS

a

b

c

d

I see many instructors who seem to get a bit obsessed with their pupils' hand and clubhead position at the frame c position of figure 22 and completely overlook the fact that the students aren't making a fundamentally sound turn. It's far more important that the body motions learned in the torso drill are repeated. The photos in figure 23 show that I am indeed using the learned body motions as I swing the club.

My clubhead, hands, and arms are all attached to the body. If my torso makes a wrong or unbalanced move, the effect is greatly magnified out at the clubhead.

Keep the Right Arm and Shoulder Relaxed

The photos in figure 24 illustrate the way in which your right arm can inhibit the free turning of your shoulders at the start of the golf swing. The lines on the right photo show that the angle has been reduced compared to the left-arm-only takeaway. My right shoulder clearly has not turned as far behind my spine in the one-handed takeaway. Prior to initiating the two-handed takeaway, I must remember to relax all tension in my right hand, arm, and shoulder. If I start the swing with too much tension,

FIGURE 24: TURN-INHIBITING INFLUENCE OF RIGHT ARM

a   b

my turn will be restricted early on, and the collapsing of the angle between my left arm and shoulder line will cost me power unless I correct
it with a very strong shoulder turn later in the backswing.

A common feature of the greatest, classic golf swings, such as those
of Jones, Snead, Hogan, Faldo, and Woods, is the abruptness with which
the right shoulder gets turned behind the spine at the very start of the
swing. This can only be accomplished if the entire upper right side of
your body is very relaxed during the takeaway. The sooner in the backswing that your right shoulder gets turned behind your spine, the less
complicated will be the motion required to deliver a powerful blow to
the golf ball. One of the goals of both the torso drill and the left-arm-only
drill is to train your upper body to this early shoulder turn.

All top-notch players will tell you that they can sense, by the time
their hands are hip high on the backswing, whether or not a good shot
will result. Listed below are a number of actions that are *not* present in a
successful takeaway:

- ➤ Your head has not moved.
- ➤ Your left arm has not broken.
- ➤ Your right leg has not moved laterally.
- ➤ There is no swaying.
- ➤ You have not taken over the swing with wrist action.
- ➤ You have not lifted the club.

Each and every body motion in the above list, when it occurs, represents
avoidance of doing the work of the turn. The likelihood that these destructive motions will occur is increased tremendously by improper grip
and posture and, to an equal degree, by excess muscle tension, especially in the right side of your upper body.

Don't Imitate Unusual Elements of Great Players' Swings

Undoubtedly the most controversial element of the takeaway relates to
squareness of the clubface during the first foot or two of the swing. As I
mentioned earlier, the idiosyncratic square takeaway of Nicklaus's early

swing spawned the "Square to Square" phenomenon, a classic example of the golf industry promoting what is actually a flaw in a great player's swing as a revolutionary new way to swing the club.

Here's what Jack had to say on the subject in his book titled *The Full Swing*:

> With the old swing, I wanted to see the clubhead travel directly back from the ball along a rearward extension of the target line for at least a foot before my gradually increasing upper-body turn moved the clubhead to the inside. Today, . . . I want to see the face of the club opening quickly relative to the target line and continuing to open as it disappears.

At this point I have adequately described the physical motions involved during a fundamentally sound takeaway. But what about the mental side? In *Golf—The Winning Formula*, Nick Faldo describes his thoughts about the takeaway:

> Knees. They very definitely resist the turn. . . . Legs. These just maintain the feeling of resistance. . . . Hips. The right hip is sent back and round me to move round in the rest of the backswing. No lateral movement at all. . . . Shoulders. The right shoulder, like the right hip turns back behind me. . . . Arms. These are pulled into movement by the body turn, but no independent feeling of their own yet. . . . Elbows. The elbows move away in harmony with everything else, the right one tucking in and down a touch. . . . Hands. These are passive for the moment.

Faldo has it right. His comments on the right shoulder and hip are of particular significance and should help the average player make an adequate turn. But like Hogan before him, I think Nick has omitted mention of the subtle action of the right knee, which moves backward slightly before assuming its fixed position. Of course you can take it away, like Trevino, and still hit the golf ball, but what I am after here is simplicity and economy of motion, driven by the belief that a simple swing must be the easiest to learn for the greatest number of golfers.

FIGURE 25: CLUBFACE OPENS NATURALLY ON TAKEAWAY

a

b

c

The sequence in figure 25 shows clearly that the clubface is fanning open as I begin my takeaway. I am not forcing it to open: This happens naturally because I'm turning my upper body about my spine. Any attempt to force the clubface to remain square up to frame c will result in too steep a shoulder turn and a flying right elbow. These two evils greatly increase the difficulty of producing a solid and square blow to the ball at impact.

Here is what Bobby Jones had to say about the takeaway:

If you will stand out on the first tee some Sunday afternoon you will find that you will be able to divide almost all your friends into two groups, merely by the manner in which they start their backswings. You will find that nearly all of them originate the motion solely with the wrists but in two ways. One group will be the "lifters" and the other will be the "rollers". Occasionally you will find a "swinger" but he will be a better player.[4]

The method put forth in this chapter will teach you to become a swinger. Learn it well and you will *neither a lifter nor a roller be.*

---

[4] *Bobby Jones on Golf*

8

Storing
Power
at the Top

The most physically demanding phase of the golf swing begins as your hands reach hip level on the backswing. The more you have gotten your right shoulder turned behind you at this point, the less effort you'll need to complete the powerful coil—but in any case the hardest work of the turn begins here. In the full golf swing, the shoulders go through a rotation of about ninety degrees relative to the axis of rotation, the spine. At the same time, your left arm achieves a rotation of approximately forty degrees about its hinge point at your left shoulder.

The solid lines between my shoulders in the figure 26 photos illustrate a shoulder turn of just about ninety degrees—not too bad for a fifty-six-year-old. During my senior year in college I fought a back problem that would cause lower-back pain as I tried to get into position for putts. I developed a daily regimen of early-morning stretches, which I continue to this day.

The dotted lines in the photos show that my left arm has a total angle change of about 130 degrees, 90 degrees of which result from being attached to my left shoulder and the other 40 degrees being rotation about my shoulder joint. The change in angle between the solid and dotted lines indicates the relative rotation of my left arm about my shoulder joint.

For reference, I have drawn a vertical line down from the back of my head. At the top of this 3-wood backswing, my head has moved a couple of inches away from the target and has rotated about ten or fifteen degrees. Some head rotation is inevitable. Indeed, several great players, Watson and Nicklaus included, have included this head rotation in their address position. I have experimented with this presetting of the head and found it disorientating, requiring a great deal of practice to be assimilated into my normal swing. The lateral motion of my head is noticeable. Many top-notch players coexist with a small amount of this lateral motion. The classic swings of Hogan, Snead, and Woods have contained almost no lateral head movement as the club is swung to the top of the backswing. It is not particularly helpful to become to obsessed with eliminating all lateral head movement. If your weight is on the inside of your right foot at the top, any small motion that occurs will not cause major problems.

At the top of the backswing, muscular potential energy or potential power is stored in many forms:

FIGURE 26A & B: POSITION AT TOP WITH 3-WOOD, FRONT VIEW

a   b

➤ Gravitational.

➤ Hinging of your wrists.

➤ Rotation of your forearms.

➤ Rotation of your hips against your braced legs.

➤ Rotation of your shoulders against your restraining hips, which are, in turn, braced by your legs.

➤ Rotation of your left arm around your left shoulder joint against the restraint of your shoulders.

➤ Final stretching of your right shoulder as your left arm reaches the top of the backswing.

➤ Stretched muscles along your inner right thigh restraining further hip rotation and preventing your right knee from straightening.

➤ Lower leg muscles maintaining ground pressure along the inner edge of your right foot.

As the backswing reaches the point at which your hands are hip level, the real work begins. All the common mantras become suddenly very hard to obey.

GOLF'S LIST OF DON'TS

➤ Don't lift your head.

➤ Don't move your head laterally.

➤ Don't let your weight sway to the outside of your right foot.

➤ Don't break your left arm.

➤ Don't change the spine angle you started the swing with.

➤ Don't let your right leg go straight.

Allowing any one of these prohibited actions causes some of the power you are attempting to store to dissipate. Critical muscles lose tension, and clubhead speed and control are lost. In most golfers the spirit is willing but the body is weak, is too tense, or lacks flexibility.

So let's say you're willing to practice and make some changes to achieve the distance you've always coveted. Just how do you go about it? I'll assume that you can comfortably achieve the position shown below in frame a of figure 27 when you're at the top with a wedge. But if you try to make a longer swinger, it all goes badly wrong.

The Swing Doesn't Change Much

The fundamental problem with midhandicappers who actually manage to get into the position shown in frame a of figure 27 is that they don't recognize just how close they are to the Promised Land. Like a hiker lost in the mountains with the base camp just over the next hill, they head off in another direction and never reach the goal. As soon as they grab a longer club, especially the driver, they start trying to do "other" things, like getting to parallel or reaching for more extension, and they immediately begin to violate one or more of the items on the list of don'ts.

Very little actually happens in between the positions shown in frames a and b. Of course I addressed the 3-wood with a more closed and wider stance than for the wedge, and the club is much longer. Other than that,

FIGURE 27A & B: SIMILARITY OF POSITIONS AT TOP, WEDGE VERSUS 3-WOOD

a   b

I have simply coiled my shoulders another ten degrees or so and driven my left arm another five degrees in its rotation about the shoulder joint. And in doing this, I haven't violated any of the list of don'ts.

Actually, the strain of reaching this power position has moved my head just a couple of inches away from the target, but not enough to cause consistently serious problems. This small shift does make me slightly more prone to spin out at impact, but also it lessens the chance of a reverse pivot. Some very good golfers have won major championships while slightly violating only one of these don'ts. I cannot think of any golfer who has won on tour while simultaneously violating more than one.

Many—indeed, most—of the golf instruction books I have seen either state or imply that it should be relatively easy for the average golfer to add lots of distance. A simple tweak here and there and *poof*—it's a done deal. No sweat! Yet there's not even the slightest bit of real evidence that the process actually is easy! Obviously, we golfers just cannot resist a tall and improbable story, especially when we are the heroes of the yarn.

The misleading ease of very good golf swings and the yearning for the quick fix conspire to lead us astray from a realistic comprehension of the underlying physical difficulty of hitting a drive 270 yards in the air. Most midhandicap golfers remain so not because they lack inherent athletic ability, physical strength, or flexibility, but because they are very confused about swing fundamentals and have been led to suspect that a small, insightful tip can convert a 15 to a 2 handicapper. The first step along the path to improvement is to truly understand the challenge presented and commit the time and physical energy and mental determination needed to succeed.

The photos in figure 28 show a 3-wood swing, beginning in frame a at the end of the takeaway as discussed in the last chapter. It's important to remember that these photos are "dynamic" snapshots of a body in motion and, as a result, the principles of static equilibrium do not strictly apply. (Sorry about that—the engineer in me got loose for a moment.) To put it in plain English, look at frame d, in which I have placed a circle estimating the center of mass of my body. According to this center of mass

FIGURE 28: THE WORK OF THE TURN REVEALED

a

b

c

d

applied to a static picture, you'd expect about 60 percent of my weight to be on my right foot. Yet dynamically, at the top of the backswing, nearly all my weight is on my right foot and my left foot is just a prop, as Sam Snead put it.

Frame 28d shows my firmly braced right leg, angled inward, resisting the coil. This leg is loaded up both by my body's gravitational weight and the effort of decelerating the coil—that is, of bringing to a halt the momentum my upper body has built up during the turn. Seen in real time, the swing of a good golfer appears deceptively effortless. The photos in figure 28 argue otherwise. There is real work going on here. It is not at all easy to stay in the correct posture and not violate the lists of don'ts while coiling to a position of fully stored power. A lot of mediocre golfers achieve a useful approximation of the position of frame a and then just bail out to a relatively impotent position at the top. Yet if you return to figure 27 for a moment and study the two positions, you must admit the great similarities. You are, indeed, almost there if you can get to the wedge position correctly. What you need is a practical set of instructions, some stretching exercises to increase your flexibility, and a training drill to allow you to execute this theoretically simple—but in actual fact not-so-easy—completion of the backswing. The instructions and the drills are in the next chapter, "The Coiling Drill." A couple of South Africaners, Gary Player[5] and Ernie Els,[6] have presented exercises for increasing flexibility and strengthening golf muscles. I recommend that you incorporate a set of exercises into your daily routine. If you have not yet done so, now would be a great time. You will greatly reduce the chances of ending up on the chiropractor's table.

With excess clothing stripped away in figure 29, the power stored at the top of the modern golf swing is seen more clearly. My legs brace and restrain further windup of my torso. Because my left arm is straight, I have maintained the widest arc possible without causing excess head movement, and I have stretched my back and torso muscles to their

---

[5] *Golf Begins at 50*
[6] *Ernie Els' Guide to Golf Fitness*

FIGURE 29: AT THE TOP

a

b

c

FIGURE 30: OVERHEAD VIEW OF BODY'S WINDUP AT TOP

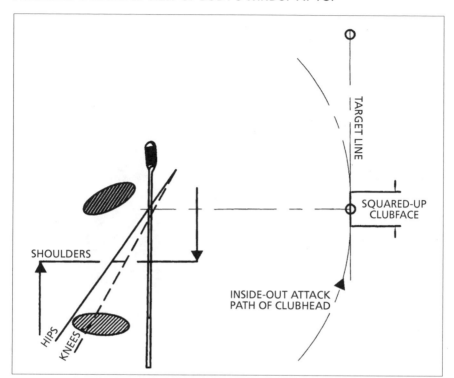

practical limit. Power is stored from ground up, starting from the anchor my feet provide, particularly my right foot.

Figure 30 shows from above the progressive windup of my knees, hips, and shoulders. The solid line is the target line; the dashed line runs through my knees, and the dotted line through my hips; the phantom line represents the ninety-degree rotation of my shoulders.

The arrows represent the torsional windup generated by my full shoulder turn about the spine. Because my feet are anchored to the ground and my legs are bracing, the line through my kneecaps rotates only about twenty or thirty degrees. My hips have a bit more freedom, being farther from the anchor point, and they are rotated about thirty-five to forty-five degrees relative to the target line.

9

The Coiling Drill

M y late friend Jason Mannes taught me this drill. He told me that Nick Price had learned it from David Leadbetter, and that Price liked it so well he was tempted to originate his golf swing from its starting position. I have not researched the authenticity of Jason's account of the origin of this drill, but I have found it, with minor changes, to be one of the best for ingraining the necessary muscle memory for the second half of the backswing.

The coiling drill, shown here using an 8-iron, is begun with the body at rest in the position shown in figure 31a. At this stage my shoulders have rotated about thirty-five degrees, my hips about twenty degrees, and the line through my knees about ten degrees when compared to the address position. The clubface has rotated ninety degrees; the shaft is just below parallel with the ground. This stage of the golf swing is reached primarily by torso rotation.

I begin this drill from position a by continuing the rotation of my right shoulder behind me. My left arm is pulled across my chest by this motion, with my hands moving on a path aimed at my right shoulder. Many golfers bail out just at this point, allowing the hands to start lifting up, aimed more or less at the right ear.

In figure 31b the hinging of my hands has begun, as shown by the increased angle between my left arm and the shaft. This hinging action tends to "pin" my right forearm against my chest, keeping me in tight

FIGURE 31: THE COILING DRILL

a: start at rest in this position

b: first stage of coil; hands go toward right shoulder

c: shoulder rotation almost complete; head and spine very steady

d: top of backswing

e: dropping into the slot   **f**: pure at impact and beyond

coil. This coil pulls against my braced legs to begin to stretch the muscles across my back. At this point I am beginning to store real power.

Frames c and d show the continuation to the top. It's very unlikely that most golfers, just beginning this drill, will be able to reach the position shown in frame d. If you can only reach this position shown in frame c without violating the list of don'ts, that's okay. By working within this drill and doing your daily set of flexibility exercises, you will gradually increase the amount of coil in your swing. Note in frame d that only at the top of the backswing does my right elbow lift clear; the line from my shoulder to my elbow still points very much at the ground and not into the sky.

Frames e and f of figure 31 show the downswing and impact. My right elbow gets quickly reconnected to my right side as my legs and hips lead the way. Note the dramatic change in right-elbow position between frames 31d and 31e. *My right shoulder is "held back" in frame e, allowing my hands and clubhead to approach impact from an inside path.* In figures 31e and f I have added solid lines through my shoulders. The line in

31e is in line with the target, and even in 31f this line points only slightly left of target. The dotted lines indicate what happens in many mediocre and bad swings. By the time most slicers reach the positions shown, the line through the shoulders will be pointing well to the left of target, forcing a drastic cut across and the resulting slice.

Figure 32 shows a frontal view of the starting point for the coiling drill using a 3-wood. You should learn this drill with a wedge and the short irons first, and then progress to the longer clubs. Each time you consciously place yourself into the ideal position with your hands hip high on the backswing, you are ingraining the muscle memory for this position's feel. It soon will become much easier for you to sense when a normal backswing does *not* pass through this position. The vertical line coincides with the line of my spine, which is, of course, tipped out of the page at the top. The curved arrow indicates that the coiling will take place about my spine. My spine neither moves laterally nor lifts up as the coiling progresses. Most golfers seem a bit confused as to how to get into a powerful position at the top. More than anything else, it is the coiling of the torso against the braced legs that generates power

Frames a, b, and c of figure 33 show the coiling action with the 3-wood. Again, if you can only make it to the position shown in frame b without violating the list of don'ts, then make position b the top of your backswing and let your hands complete their hinging at this point. Dana Quigley just keeps cashing checks with a turn about as full as that shown in frame b. Use flexibility exercises, the torso drill, and this coiling drill to gradually increase the power stored at the top of your golf swing.

FIGURE 32: FRONTAL VIEW, COILING DRILL START POSITION

FIGURE 33: COILING DRILL, FRONTAL VIEW

a   b   c

d   e   f

This drill is not my invention, but I have changed it somewhat based on my own experience. The prevailing idea seems to be to simply move your left arm to a horizontal position without doing anything with your hips and shoulders at the start position. Done this way, it forces you to really crank your shoulders abot your spine quickly and tightly to get your hands into hitting position at the top. With experimentation, I became much more comfortable with the starting position exactly mirroring the position I want on a real swing. If you learn this drill and practice it diligently, you will improve your golf swing and hit the ball farther. The coiling drill can teach you:

> ➤ To recognize the correct position at hip height.
> ➤ To coil and store power without violating the lists of don'ts.
> ➤ To recognize physically and mentally the correct position at the top.

You are now well on the way to hitting the living daylights out of the golf ball.

10

Dropping the Hammer

We come now to what is, without question, golf's most confused issue: how to initiate the downswing. There is no need here for a new theory to add to the confusion; the great golfers and instructors have taken care of that very nicely. Snead replanted his left heel. Hogan says he spun his hips. Faldo says the first move is in the left shoulder. Jimmy Ballard says the right knee should drive forward.

Happily, there are some elements of agreement among all great players and teachers:

> ➤ The ball should be struck on an inside-out path, squaring up at impact.
> ➤ Your arms must get reconnected to your torso and not get left behind.
> ➤ Casting (releasing the wrist cock like a fly-casting fisherman) from the top of the backswing must be avoided.
> ➤ The wrist cock should be retained until just prior to impact.
> ➤ Your weight should be nearly all transferred to your left foot prior to impact.
> ➤ Your left leg should not straighten until you are past impact.
> ➤ Your right elbow should very nearly touch your right hipbone as your hands reach hip level on the downswing.

So given all this agreement, how can such confusion prevail? At the core of this tempest in a teapot lie the subtle differences in the fully coiled position achieved by golf's recognized "greatest" swings.

It's the Different Lengths of Backswings That Cause the Confusion

Figure 34 shows two identical photos of my swing at the top with the driver. In frame a I have drawn a black line indicating a position of reduced left-arm rotation that would be associated with a shorter swing. If I were to stop my backswing here, the effects on my right forearm, elbow, and upper-arm positions are indicated by the white lines. The effect on my right elbow is dramatic, and the effort needed to get this elbow and my arms reconnected to my right side during the downswing has been lessened. My chances of getting ahead with the hips, of "not waiting for it," of making a disconnected swing have also been reduced. I can drive my legs and hips very aggressively into the shot without getting my arms "stuck" behind me. The swings of Ben Hogan and Tom Lehman are good examples of this shorter backswing. The accuracy that results made them both great U.S. Open players.

In frame b I have again used the solid black line to represent a hypothetical left-arm position at the top; the white solid lines show the effect on my right arm. Sam Snead got into something close to this position by letting his hips rotate farther and by letting his left heel be pulled off the ground. I have indicated the change in hip and leg positions by the solid and dotted lines in frame b. Tiger Woods, Phil Mickelson, and many other modern players are able to achieve this position while keeping the left heel grounded. It's very obvious from observing the hypothetical position in frame b that the lower body must be much more patient as the downswing begins to allow the right arm to get reconnected and not get "stuck" as the hips spin out too soon.

The extra hip motion that Snead and Nicklaus allowed in their swings adds complexity. As the downswing is initiated, the left heel *must* first be returned to the ground, and the left hip and the left knee *must* return to the positions shown by the dotted lines; then they have to slow down and wait as the right arm is getting simultaneously reconnected to the right side. Because of the length of the backswing, the right arm has a very long way to go before it passes through the position sketched in frame a. The built-up velocity of the arms and clubhead as it passes

FIGURE 34: EFFECTS OF SHORT BACKSWING VERSUS LONG

a: effects of shorter swing   b: effects of longer swing

through this spot makes the longer swing more powerful, but there is also a whole lot more to go wrong.

The photos in figure 35 are useful because there is a club on the ground behind me next to my left hip to use for comparison. I have added a white line to make this club more noticeable. In frame a I am nearing the top. My lower body initiates the downswing even as the clubhead is setting into its maximum angle. The first move in my downswing is a simultaneous start on the clearing of my left hip and a slight drive forward of my legs off the anchored right foot. The start of this unwinding while my left arm and clubhead are still traveling their last bit to the top further stretches the muscles across my back. I can really feel this additional stretch in the vicinity of my left shoulder and upper left arm. As this hip rotation begins, it's imperative not to let your right knee, hip, or shoulder be pushed out toward the ball by this rotation. They must hang back.

In frames b and c the continued driving forward of my right hip is apparent by comparing my hip position to the white lines. My hips are also

FIGURE 35: INITIATING THE DOWNSWING

a: nearing top

b: left hip and knee begin reversal

c: lower body drive continues; arms pulling down

d: continuation of hips squaring and driving forward and arms pulling downward

continuing to square up, making them appear broader in this view and tending to mask their forward motion. This motion of the hips toward the target is a critical part of the golf swing. If I were to merely spin my left hip without this forward drive of my lower body, then my right hip and shoulder would be kicked out toward the ball and I would be forced into a cut-across position. In frame c I have also added a black line showing where my left arm was in the previous frame. I have begun to pull the club downward with my left arm while driving my right elbow back toward the right hip in synchronization with my hips driving forward and my left hip continuing to clear. I can feel a push off my right foot, starting in frame b and continuing in c. As I pull downward with my left arm, the amount of wrist cock actually increases a bit, thereby "loading up" for the "late hit."

In frame d my lower body has continued to drive forward slightly. The squaring of my hips continues as my arms are racing to catch up and get my right elbow reconnected to my right side.

By frame d I have completed the reconnection of the right elbow to the right side. My right shoulder and right hip and my hands are still held back very much on an inside path. The forward motion of my hips has been sufficient to get my weight more than half transferred to my left foot. I am now continuing to drive off my right foot and pulling with my left hip and left arm as hard as I possibly can. Once into this position, there is little left to go wrong. I can hit the golf ball as hard as I am able. The ball will be hit solidly and it will go long and straight.

In frame d my weight is firmly planted on my left foot. My hips have driven forward enough so that my left leg will not straighten until impact is completed. My hips are now parallel to the target line. Only *now* do some of the hinging of my wrists and the rotation of my left forearm begin to be released.

Some of the reasons for the confusion surrounding the initiation of the downswing are made obvious by the photos and the discussion of this chapter. If you have a short backswing that features very little lift of your right elbow from your chest at the top of the backswing, you won't have a serious reconnection problem. As you start the downswing, you can very shortly begin spinning your left hip as fast as possible. Hogan said that at the start of the downswing, he spun his hips as fast as he possibly could while simultaneously driving his hips forward to shift his weight to his left foot. There can be little doubt that he did exactly this, time and again, along with an extraordinary amount of driving of both knees toward the target. But this does not make it a correct action or swing thought for a taller player or one with a much longer backswing.

Snead had to initiate the downswing by replanting his left heel and pulling down with his arms to get reconnected. The most extreme example of this waiting for reconnection is the incredible swing of John Daly. Because of John's amazing length of coil at the top, his hips, after driving forward to shift some weight to his left foot and squaring up, appear in stop-action shots to stop altogether while his arms get reconnected. An individual must have an exquisite sense of timing to pull off such a maneuver. I would never attempt to teach a midhandicapper to swing like John Daly, or that the bowlegged "Snead squat" is an essential part of every golf swing. There is actually a movement afoot in today's golf instruction community promoting the Snead squat. This is classic example of the business of golf instruction and promotion always needing new and exciting techniques. A great player's idiosyncrasy is promoted as an essential ingredient of everyone's golf swing.

As elegant as Sam Snead's swing was, it probably suffered rather than benefited from the squat. The bowleggedness appeared because Sam was a little lax in getting his weight transferred to his left foot at the start of the downswing. This would later cause his left leg to snap straight at impact, especially with the driver. When the left leg goes straight too soon at or just before impact, the clubhead path is affected and pulled inside the target line on the follow-through. Obviously, this was not an insurmountable problem for the winningest player of all time. I just suspect he would have won even more tournaments without it.

Figure 36 shows from behind the positions of frames a and d of figure 35. In frame b are a pair of vertical white lines illustrating that my hipbones are essentially parallel to the target at this point. Most average golfers have already spun out at this point—their hips have outraced

FIGURE 36: DROPPING INTO THE SLOT

a: top of backswing   b: right shoulder and hip held back

their arms, and their buttocks are already rotated around facing the camera. I have drawn a solid black line to show just how much my right shoulder is still held back. It's very clear in frame b that I'm in excellent position to deliver a square blow to the golf ball, approaching it on an inside-out path. The proper transition from the position in frame a to that in frame b is one of the very most elusive elements of the golf swing to convey to the midhandicapper. I believe that it's less a question of athletic skills than of understanding what's supposed to be going on. And it's the pervasive notion of spinning the hips to start the downswing that contributes most mightily to this misunderstanding.

Put Your Right Hand in Your Right Pocket!

In figure 36b I have added another dotted black line to indicate where my left arm had been in frame a, and an arrow showing the path my hands have followed in making this transition. This path is much more

FIGURE 37A & B: INTO THE HITTING ZONE

vertical than it is horizontal. The vertical element of the transition is akin to a two-handed hammer blow, leading to the title of this chapter. As I was taught at the age of five, I am attempting to "put my right hand in my pocket." Clearly impossible as this may be, the concept is very useful in the creation of an inside-out approach to the golf ball.

Figure 37 summarizes the desired body and clubhead positions as you enter the hitting zone. The main elements are:

➤ Right elbow reconnected to right side.
➤ Knees and hips driven toward target.
➤ Right shoulder held back.
➤ Wrist cock retained.
➤ Hips parallel to target.
➤ Clubhead well behind my body.

Achieve this position and a good shot is a done deal!

11

Impact and Follow-Through

N ow it's time to hit the golf ball. All your work and energy and concentration thus far have hopefully brought you into a balanced position, poised to be pure at impact. The clubhead is racing through the air. The final elements of stored power—the wrist cock and the left-forearm rotation—are about to be released. This is clearly happening in the transition from frame a to frame b of figure 38, in which there is relatively small change in arm positions but a very large change in clubhead position. The forward motion of my hips at the early stages of the downswing is very apparent here, because all my weight is now on my left foot, and the heel of my right foot begins to come off the ground. Only in frame b do my buttocks begin to appear to thc camera's eye.

Much of this book deals with a specific way to swing the club. I believe the principles put forth in this book are those most likely to help the greatest number of golfers. I have always been attracted to the "classic" swing with its clean lines, economy of effort, and simplicity of motion. The golf ball, waiting on the tee in frame b, doesn't give a damn about all this stuff. You can pick the club up like Miller Barber, loop it like Jim Furyk, or deliver a consistent cut like Trevino or Lietske: It doesn't matter as long as you get into something close to the positions shown in frames a and b of figure 38.

FIGURE 38A & B: ATTACKING THE BALL FROM THE INSIDE PATH

FIGURE 39: CHASING DOWN THE TARGET LINE

a: repeated   b: impact and chase

When discussing iron play—and particularly short iron play—good players often talk about having a feeling of holding back the release of their wrists at impact. But when I reach the positions shown in figure 38 with the driver, there is no thought of holding back anything. Because I have successfully retained my wrist cock and left-forearm rotation until frame a, I can now let it all loose, as hard as I possibly can, while trying to keep the clubhead very square through impact.

Figure 39 dramatically illustrates just how much the clubhead attacks the golf ball from an inside path. The clubface squares up just before impact and then chases down the target line until the physics of the body begin to pull it inside. Frame b illustrates that bit of advice given by golf pros to every pupil: "Hit through the golf ball, not at it." As I make contact I am truly attempting to hit long and low, through the ball, driving the square clubface right out at the target.

Now You Can Let It Rip

This same sequence, seen face-on in figure 40, shows that in frame a, the last bit of weight transfer is occurring and that, in frame b, all my weight is on my left foot. My right elbow is tucked in against my right side. Because I have made this weight transfer by the lateral movement of my hips toward the target (as discussed in detail in the last chapter) my left leg has still not quite snapped to straight even in frame b. This allows the clubface to remain squared up beyond impact, as is clearly shown in frame b. In frame b, both arms are now fully extended. Nothing is held back.

Note the position of my head in figures 40 and 41. There is very little change of head position in any of these photos. By the time I reach the position shown in figure 41, frame b, my head is about to be rotated by the momentum of my right shoulder, but it has still not moved. If you go back and check my head position in figures 38 and 39, you will also see no head movement from the target line perspective. My head does not lift up because my left leg retains some flex at impact; it only goes dead straight well beyond impact.

As the follow-through continues in frame a of figure 42, the clubface naturally rolls over to a closed position. Note the extension of my right

FIGURE 40: DELIVERING THE LATE HIT

a: unleashing full power

b: clubface square through impact

FIGURE 41: STAYING LONG AND LOW BEYOND IMPACT

a: repeated

b: staying down *through* impact

FIGURE 42A & B: TRANSITION TO THE FINISH

FIGURE 43A & B: THE ON-BALANCE FINISH, EVIDENCE OF A GOOD SWING

arm and that my head is still down. Only in frame b does my head begin to rotate toward the target. Figure 43 shows the transition to the finish with my head coming forward and up, my hips turned to fully face the target, only the toe of my right foot on the ground, my right knee pointing toward the target, and my hands high.

The Finish Position Is Like a Crime Scene

Top-level golfers tend to be a bit obsessed with the finish position. It is essentially a crime scene, leaving subtle clues for the trained eye. You cannot arrive at a position like the one shown in frame b of figure 43 without having made a good pass at the ball. On poor swings the balance will be absent, with perhaps some of your weight falling back to your right foot instead of you standing tall on your left leg. This is a sure indicator that the position at the top of the backswing was weak. Or your hips may not be fully rotated, indicating a lack of drive onto your left leg early in the downswing. Or your hands may not finish high, often an indicator that you've made the dreaded casting move at the start of the downswing and cut across the ball badly.

Swings of near perfection are rare even for the greatest. There is a sensual rush associated with finishing in perfect balance on a shot flawlessly executed. Some amount of private celebration is allowed— indeed, irresistible. If you watch a touring pro long enough, you will learn his or her individual mannerisms accompanying this moment. Many, like Mark O'Meara and Tiger, will give a dashing twirl of the club. Arnie would cock his head ever so slightly as he tried to visualize the ball going in the hole. Tom Watson made a little arm swing. Tiger has added a little dance step recently, a bit of a prance with his right leg as the first step after the shot timed in conjunction with the twirl. Many others simply hold the perfect pose at the finish for a few extra seconds.

These are not conscious actions of self-congratulation. They are, rather, irrepressible manifestations of joy, small movements to try to prolong the pleasure. If you play this game long enough, amid so many shots that bring disappointment, pain, and embarrassment you will hit a very few that are actually astonishing in their excellence. Given the rarity of the event and the briefness of the sensation, some private cele-bration seems justified.

Golf is a game that takes particular vengeance on arrogance and stu-pidity. Nearly all the game's greatest champions have learned, in their own way, a deep respect for the game and their competitors. Seasoned competitors become distrustful of their own overzealous reactions, de-veloping a kind of superstitious aversion to giving themselves much credit for a good round or shot. With disaster lurking on nearly every shot, it's good practice not to invite the attention of the gods. Take your birdie and go quietly. Hold the pose, if you will, but also hold your tongue.

12

Timing the Power Hit

R ules are made to be broken," the saying goes. When teaching the game to beginners or trying to improve midhandicappers, instructors are often heard to say, "You're trying to hit it too hard," or "You must slow down and wait for the clubhead," or "Swing easy to hit it long." And yet when we observe top players hitting shots that demand another twenty or thirty yards from the club in hand, we see them making a vicious pass at the ball with every ounce of strength and clubhead speed possible, and very often pulling it off successfully. *How?* and *When?* are the questions begging answers, and timing is the key to unraveling this paradox.

In '68 I found myself twice paired with Mike Souchak, first in the U.S. Open sectional qualifier in Detroit and later in the final round of the Michigan Open. Mike was well known as a great player and a long hitter, and I was a bit mystified to find our drives side by side on hole after hole. Although I had finished well up in the '67 NCAA driving contest, I did not try to hit it long in competition, being satisfied to fly the ball 260 yards on my good drives. The answer arrived on the first par 5 in that final round, when I found myself, after a well-struck drive, forty yards behind Mr. Souchak. You see, the U.S. Open qualifier course had been very tight, and the last thing you want under those circumstances is a big number. So I played forty holes of competition with this long hitter before I ever witnessed his power firsthand. It came on a 565-yard, wide-open par 5 with minimal risk and everything to gain. Timing! Mike's swing was a bit faster than normal, and his drive into the ball with his legs more aggressive than normal, with the impact as pure as can be. Timing!

(By the way, this '68 Michigan Open—one of my best events ever—had a strange little side story to it. I almost didn't bother to compete! Every summer since I was fifteen, I had worked full time doing golf course maintenance. In '68 I was working at Pine Lake Country Club just outside Detroit, saving money for the coming school year. In mid-June the night waterer quit and I began filling in from 10 P.M. until 2 A.M. each night in addition to working the day shift. For the month leading up to the tournament, I played very little. When I played my practice round for the event, I don't think I broke 80. Discouraged, I almost didn't show up for the first round. On the opening nine of the tournament, I shot 40 and perhaps would have given up right there except for making a birdie on the ninth hole. Deciding to hang around for the second nine, I shot 31 and then made only a couple of bogeys the rest of the week.)

Timing—The Mental Side

There really aren't many occasions when hitting the golf ball as hard as you can makes much sense. But these situations do pop up now and then, and having the shot in your bag of tricks not only helps your score but also provides a big boost of confidence and enthusiasm. Here are a few of the most obvious shots where a big hit is the right choice:

- ➤ The wide-open par 5 described above.
- ➤ A very long par 4 that you are likely to bogey if you don't crush the drive—and you won't likely make more than bogey if the drive gets away from you.
- ➤ A short par 4, maybe even reachable, that opens up around the green, making the green-side recovery shot not too difficult.
- ➤ A shot over a tree of 5-iron distance—but you can only get over the tree with a 7-iron.
- ➤ A shot under a tree that must carry a hazard a long way out to have a chance to run onto the green.

> ➤ A shot from deep rough.
> ➤ A plugged lie in the bunker.

Here are a number of opposing cases where the big hit makes no sense:

> ➤ Into the wind. You impart more spin with a hard hit and are very likely to hit a wild shot. Although the best players in the world sometimes really blast a low one into the wind, controlling this shot is as difficult as it gets.
> ➤ The risk-reward ratio stinks. Many times a wild shot can be so costly it makes no sense to try it.
> ➤ You do not have a level stance. Nonlevel lies require reduced leg action and more of an arm swing—just the opposite of the requirements of the big hit. Typically you take an extra club and swing easy from nonlevel lies.
> ➤ The long drive or hard 3-wood takes you into the no-man's-land of a sixty- to eighty-yard wedge. Far better to leave it at 100 yards for your sand wedge or even 120 yards for the full pitching wedge.
> ➤ In some situations there may be little risk—but there may also be no gain. Keep it in the fairway.

The above lists may seem quite obvious and easy to obey, but as you acquire the physical skill to deliver the big hit, the temptation to use the skill indiscriminately increases. Here are a few situations in which a long drive is tempting but ill advised:

> ➤ You are really ticked off and want to blow off steam.
> ➤ You think it may demoralize your opponent.
> ➤ You want to show off your power and the round has not presented any opportunity.
> ➤ A playing partner is constantly outdriving you.
> ➤ It's a bad round already, so what the hell? Trust me, it will get worse if you start trying to kill every shot.

Golf is more a game of attrition than a contest dominated by a few outstanding shots. Make fewer dumb shots than your slightly more skilled opponent and you will win more often than you'll lose.

Timing—The Physical Side

There are two ways to hit the ball longer:

1. Deliver a more direct blow to the ball without decreasing club-head speed.
2. Increase clubhead speed without sacrificing the directness of the blow to the ball.

At impact with the driver in frame b of figure 44, my hands are swinging through the air at about 30 miles per hour and the clubhead is racing at about 110 mph. When I need to "let out the shaft," it must be done without destroying the balanced positions shown in frames a and b or else I will degrade the squareness of the blow to the ball. I do not want to deviate from my first rule of impact, the Momentum Law:

> For a given clubhead speed, the maximum possible momentum will be transferred to the golf ball when the clubhead is traveling down the intended path of the target and the clubhead is

FIGURE 44A & B: LETTING OUT THE SHAFT

perfectly square to the target during the milliseconds that the ball remains in contact with the clubhead.

So I want to pass through exactly these same dynamic positions but with:

1. More velocity of my hands through the air.
2. Increased power of release of my wrist cock and forearm rotation.
3. Increased clubhead speed, square and on target.

Some of the advice appearing in the instruction books of the great golfers is good advice for aspiring young players who are going to devote their lives to improvement. This same advice can often be ruinous for the weekend golfer. A classic example, the notion that you should learn first to hit the ball hard and later to control your shots, leads midhandicappers astray from the first law of impact. Unless you are a person of exceptional athletic skills, you really must first learn to arrive at impact in a useful approximation of the position shown in frame b, and *then* work on adding distance.

When sportswriters heaped praise on John Wooden as the greatest basketball coach of all time, he would often reply, "You can't make chicken salad without the chicken"—meaning, of course, that the talented players, not the coaching, were the essential ingredient. In your quest for longer drives, you should realize that arriving at something near the correct impact position is the "chicken" needed for long and straight driving. As you continue building your own "chicken salad" of power driving, I am assuming that you've improved to the stage where you can, when swinging easy, hit the ball a reasonable distance and fairly straight. Trying to superimpose the instructions that follow onto a seriously flawed position at impact will only make you worse.

Relax and Focus to Hit the Long Ball

As you approach a tee box where it makes good sense to add an extra twenty or thirty yards to your normal drive, begin to visualize the ball exploding from the clubface and streaking directly on target. You should have a sense of gathering all your strength for the moment of impact. I actually have a sense that my body is getting bigger and stronger in preparation. At the same time, relaxation and focus must begin. Take at least two deep breaths, and try to empty your mind of all thoughts except that image of explosion at impact. As you take the deep breaths, consciously relax your neck and shoulder muscles and, even more so, the muscles in your right arm and shoulder. Without freedom in your swing, the long hit will not happen, and if you have too much muscle tension you won't have freedom.

Clear Your Mind of All Mechanical Swing Thoughts

Tee the ball slightly higher and position it slightly farther ahead in your stance. The swing you're about to make will feature more forward leg drive than usual (you don't have to think about this—it'll just happen), and this puts the bottom of the arc of the swing a bit farther forward. Clear your mind of all mechanical swing thoughts. Focus on swinging smoothly back and then building speed as you enter into the hitting zone. Make an extra effort to swing the clubhead long and low along the

FIGURE 45A & B: SQUARE DOWN THE TARGET LINE

target line after impact, as shown in figure 45. Note how squared to the target the clubhead remains after impact. At the moment of contact, you should feel that every ounce of strength your body possesses is being imparted to the golf ball. And also at the moment of impact, you should be asserting every bit of your willpower that this golf ball is going to go *exactly* where you want it to go.

When you pull the extra-long hit off successfully, realize that you have captured a bit of "lightning in a bottle." Don't go to this well too often or it will go dry. On my very best swinging days, I may use this shot twice at most, if the occasions arise. I have learned by painful experience that it won't work at all on days when I'm struggling with my swing.

The power hit is one of the true joys of the game. You won't learn it by just reading about it and then trying it during the round. During practice sessions, when you reach a moment when you're hitting well, attempt this shot a couple of times with the driver or imagine that you need a long and low 4-iron, or an 8-iron blasted high over a tree. In every practice session hit a few shots very hard using the method described here. This will help you learn to synchronize your swing at the more intense level needed for the power hit.

3

Overcoming Fear of the Driver: Drills and Exercises

N ow you have all the knowledge you need to hit the driver long and straight, so let's begin to make it a reality. There are several very practical tips toward eliminating fear of the driver:

> ➤ Learn the proper impact position. It's similar for every club in the bag.
> ➤ Learn the proper position entering the hitting zone. Again, this is similar for every club in the bag.
> ➤ Practice using a choked-down grip on the driver and a shorter swing, then graduate to the full power swing.
> ➤ Commit to using the driver on the course when it makes sense. Quit automatically bailing out to the 3-wood.
> ➤ Develop a routine and then stick with it.
> ➤ Learn to swing with a positive image of impact and ball flight.

Figure 46 illustrates the similar positions near impact for the extreme ends of the shot spectrum, driver and wedge. When you were taught to hit a wedge, the pro told you to open your stance and put nearly all your

FIGURE 46A & B: THE SIMILAR POSITIONS OF IMPACT

weight on your left foot. All you're really doing is placing yourself in the correct impact posture for this shot. Because the backswing is so restricted on short shots, you want to open your stance to get your left hip cleared out to the same position it will achieve with the driver. Stand in front of the mirror with a wedge in your hand and place yourself exactly into the near-impact position shown in figure 46. Then repeat with the driver. *Memorize these positions!*

13

The Snowplow Drills

To see a world in a grain of sand,
And a heaven in a wild flower,
Hold Infinity in the palm of your hand,
And Eternity in an hour.

—William Blake, "Auguries of Innocence"

E very shot that is truly struck is something of a miracle of hand-eye coordination, yet nearly all of us possess this innate coordination because of our evolutionary history. The uncoordinated among our ancestors would not have fared well fighting saber-toothed tigers with tree branches. Granted, striking the perfect drive ranks high on degree-of-difficulty charts, akin in nature to an eagle dropping from the sky to strafe the water and grab an unlucky salmon. Nonetheless, miracles of coordination are bred into us. The eagle has the great advantage of not being analytical. It has no theories about the initiation of the dive or whether its left claw or right claw leads the way into the salmon. It doesn't have an oversized brain to spoil its lunch.

I was probably no more than eight or nine years old the first time I was asked for advice on how to hit a golf ball. So I now have almost fifty years of experience in giving sincere and well-intended advice that has only on rare occasions been received and put into practice with anything like success. Were the nuggets of information I shared bad? No, they were never much different from the instruction you might receive from your local pro or from reading the tips in *Golf Magazine.*

Adding to the frustration of the aspiring midhandicapper is the irrefutable fact that the golf swing of an accomplished pro just looks so damn easy. How could anything so difficult look so easy? Well, remember the eagle, and recall that the codes embedded in the double helix of our DNA are nearly identical. Tweak a gene here and there and we would be soaring the mountaintops instead of chunking delicate chip shots.

In this chapter the most fundamental swing drills of golf are introduced. You may find it a bit odd in a book about the driver to find chipping drills and wedge drills. I call them the snowplow drills because they are as fundamental to golf as learning the snowplow is to skiing.

These drills will help you to:

> ➤ Learn to hit down and through the golf ball.
> ➤ Eliminate the tendency to try to lift the ball with your right hand.
> ➤ Deliver a great deal of power to the ball with a very short swing.
> ➤ Learn to hit the ball squarely.

But the most important lesson these drills have to offer is to allow you to recognize, physically and intellectually, the proper position at impact. Once you have learned to execute these drills properly, I would suggest using them once a month for about ten to fifteen minutes. This will keep your chipping and wedge play sharp and reinforce your correct sense of impact.

The setup for the first drill is seen in the first photo of figure 47. The stance is open—my lower body has been rotated about thirty degrees toward the target. My shoulders, however, are parallel to the target. The ball is played back in the stance, just about opposite my right toe. My weight is entirely on my left foot. My right foot provides balance but takes none of my body's weight.

My knees are flexed in a comfortable, athletic stance. One desired result of this setup position is that my left hand is well ahead of the golf ball at address. It is obvious from the first glance at my address position that I will be delivering a descending blow to the golf ball. With no right hand

FIGURE 47: LEFT-HAND CHIPPING DRILL

a: left hand well forward

b: left arm straight; forearm rotates clubface open

c: left arm pulls, clubface open

d: descending blow, clubhead square at impact

FIGURE 47: LEFT-HAND CHIPPING DRILL (CONTINUED)

e: square through impact   f: square to finish

to lift the ball and by pulling the clubhead downward into the ball (as seen in frame d), the golf ball leaps upward into flight the instant after impact. This drill should, once and forever, convince you that the ball is not scooped or lifted into flight by your right hand!

If you struggle at first with this drill, do not abandon it—the "world in a grain of sand" from which the rest of a good golf swings evolves. The most common error with this drill is that—the left hand feeling weak and not in complete control—the golfer radically strengthens the left-hand grip. You must avoid this error! Only by taking the normal left-hand grip will you begin to sense the correct impact position.

Figure 48 shows the same drill from the rear view. Note in frame b that the clubhead swings open quickly on the takeaway and that, in frame c, the left thumb is pointed away from the target. The takeaway motion combines a rotation of the left forearm—the elbow does not rotate—with a level cocking of the left wrist. That is, the back of your left hand remains in the same plane as your left forearm.

FIGURE 48: SAME AS FIGURE 47 FROM REAR VIEW

a: proper left-hand grip

b: clubface rolls open

c: thumb points back

d: left arm pulls down, club attacks from inside

FIGURE 48: SAME AS FIGURE 47 FROM REAR VIEW (CONTINUED)

e: descending blow lifts ball   f: clubface square through impact

It's difficult to overstate the importance of being able to execute this simple drill correctly. I have a number of friends who are relatively low handicappers, capable of shooting in the low 70s on their best days, and yet they're extremely frustrated by their general lack of distance and consistency. In each case the root cause of the problem is cutting across the golf ball at impact. Sad to say, these friends, will never produce the distance or consistency they covet without learning to deliver a square blow to the ball.

If you think about the most common bits of advice, most are illustrated in the photos of this chapter:

- ➤ Keep your head down.
- ➤ Hit down and through the ball.
- ➤ Follow through to the target.
- ➤ Keep your left arm straight.

And finally, the most confusing of them all:

- ➤ Let the clubhead do the work.

Let the clubhead do the work? What can this mean? Figure 49 illustrates the concept best. What the pros are really trying to convey is that your hands should remain relaxed and your wrists rotated and cocked until just before impact. Then the weight of the clubhead will cause it to catch up naturally at impact—*if* you don't try to force the issue. There is an element of trust involved here that the average golfer with an imperfect grip cannot seem to accept and put into action. Note the very small change in hand position from frame a to b compared to the relatively large change in clubhead position between these frames. I am clearly letting the clubhead do the work!

Because I have retained the wrist cock and the forearm rotation in a relaxed manner, the clubhead is allowed to accelerate and square up through impact naturally. I have not consciously sent any instructions to my left hand to make this happen. Because I have a proper grip with my left hand and have swung into the proper hitting position in frame a, it just happens!

The principal act of faith involved here is to keep your left hand moving and accelerating through the impact zone, delivering a descending

FIGURE 49A & B: CLUBHEAD DOING THE WORK

blow to the golf ball and trusting the loft of the clubhead to get the ball airborne.

What do you do with your hands? This is undoubtably the question I have been asked with the most frequency during the last forty-five years. My standard answer—"I am not much aware of my hands"—is truthful but not very helpful for the novice or average player.

The photos of this chapter exhibit how my left hand leads the way through the impact area on the short chip shot. Although the hinging action on the takeaway is delayed a bit on longer swings, there is no difference in the impact zone for this hand action. By mastering the correct left-arm and -hand action on short chips, you will sense a crispness of ball striking that you may not have ever felt before.

Now you're ready to extend the left-arm-only drill to the three-quarter wedge shot. As you examine frames a and b of figure 50, you will note that much more than the length of swing has changed.

FIGURE 50: TRANSITION TO FULL SWING

a: top of swing, basic drill, chip

b: top of swing, advanced drill, three-quarter pitching wedge

In frame a my body's weight is centered entirely on my left foot, and my left arm and shoulders rotate perhaps twenty-five degrees from the address position. By the time the swing has reached the length needed for a three-quarter wedge shot, all the elements of the full swing are present. My left arm has rotated about 110 degrees from the address position, and my shoulders have rotated about 80 degrees.

The windup of the upper torso in frame b needs anchor points to react to this torsion. My right foot is firmly planted with the weight on the *inside* of my right foot. You can readily see this because *my right knee is angled in slightly toward the target.* Even though frame b shows a three-quarter wedge swing with only one arm, all the elements of a powerful golf swing are now in place: a nearly full shoulder turn about a steady head, a braced right leg, a full wrist cock, and a straight left arm.

Try to keep your left arm very straight. There is a kind of madness floating through the golf instruction community claiming that a straight left arm is not a vital part of the golf swing. This is utter nonsense. Yes, I can point to a few top-notch players whose left arms are less than perfectly straight at the top of a full swing, but I can assure you, these players are trying to keep their arm straight and are certainly not letting it break on purpose. The straight left arm rotated together with the shoulders about the axis of the spine is the source of power and control in the golf swing. Grossly bend this left arm on the backswing and you guarantee that your right hand and arm will take over and impair your shot.

Your Left Arm Provides Form and Structure

Golf professionals have been arguing for at least one hundred years as to whether the swing should be dominated by the right arm or the left. It seems to me rather obvious that the straight left arm provides the form and structure throughout the swing until well past impact. The photos in figure 51 show a right-arm-only version of the three-quarter wedge drill. Your right arm and shoulder could benefit from a shot of Novocain until the top of the backswing is reached. Until then, your right side can only cause problems by being too rigid or trying to become dominant.

FIGURE 51: CHANGING FOCUS OF RIGHT-ARM EFFORT DURING DOWNSWING

a: start of downswing   b: elbow reconnects

c: forearm doing work

FIGURE 52: LEFT-ARM ACTION IN IMPACT ZONE

a: left arm pulling down and through   b: descending blow drives ball into flight

When your right arm begins to act at the start of the downswing, the Novocain wears off first at the right shoulder and biceps and triceps. These muscles guide or pull your right upper arm back into contact with your right side and drive your right elbow toward your right hipbone. Your right wrist and hand are still numb. By frame b of figure 51 my right forearm begins to come alive and starts driving through toward the target. The arrow in frame c shows where my center of pressure is in my right arm at this stage of the swing. Only now in frame c does my right hand finally have something to do. *Hit it now!* Not sooner, not later, but now.

When the patiently timed release of your right side's power is guided into correct impact position by your pulling left arm, pure impact must follow. Frame a of figure 52 shows my left arm's center of pulling force located by the arrow. Note in frame a that the clubface is still quite open—

and that, in frame b, it is only well past impact that the clubhead has caught up with my left hand.

The left-handed drills illustrated in this chapter are a bit like the double helix of DNA: They carry in a compact form nearly all the information needed to produced a powerful driver swing. They also carry the genetic code for well-struck chip, iron, and every other golf shot.

14

Pitching Wedge Drills

A t Westview Golf Course I learned the game by instinct not long after learning to walk. I am told that I rode on my father's pull cart from age of three and first played a full nine holes at five. I remember milestones from then on: best score 47 at age seven, 73 at age nine—a bit of a fluke, since I took only 19 putts—63 at age fifteen. I had a bit of instruction from our pro Scotty Glascow, but mainly I learned by imitating my older brother Steve, Scotty, and the other good players at this course. I paid for my first full set of clubs with money earned from caddying, mostly for Scotty and Don Weibring. Don's son D. A. later used these clubs as his first set. During these years it was not at all unusual for me to play twenty-seven or thirty-six holes a day during the long, hot, western Illinois summer days or to be out in mid-March practicing on patches of grass just appearing from beneath the snow.

Steve, ten years older than me, began working on the course when he was fifteen. I can remember many days of riding to work with him as the sun came up, playing golf all day, and playing again with him when he got off work. The friends I made at Westview were much older and better golfers than I was at first, so in addition to acquiring a pretty colorful vocabulary for a seven-year-old, I had plenty of good and not-so-good swings to copy. Whenever we weren't actually playing, we'd hold driving contests with every club in the bag, including the putter. With the unwa-tered fairways baked in August, it could take in excess of two hundred yards to win the wedge driving contests. This could only be done with a perfect scull or by hooding the club so far back in the stance that it seemed possible the ball could hit you as it took flight. Another pastime was an up-and-down contest in which you could select the worst lie you could find for your opponent and, as an option, stomp on his ball one time to further "improve" his chances.

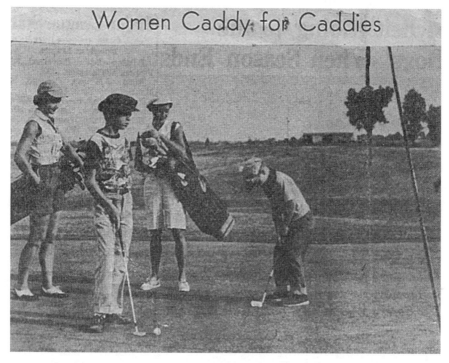

Women Caddy for Caddies

I remember this day well—it probably hooked me forever on the game. (That's me about to putt.) We must have teed off before dawn, for when we came to the eighth hole, we were playing directly into the rising sun. A typical begin-ning to a sweltering summer day on the Mississippi, the dew was still heavy on the ground. I hit a second-shot 7-iron to the short par 4. No one saw it in the glare of the sun. As we walked up to the green, we glimpsed a dew track headed straight for and stopping at the hole. My first eagle! When I caddied back then it was a lot of work for three bucks—and no one had lightweight carrying bags. Mostly leather Hot-Zs.

These are wonderful days in my memory. The dollar had real value. A dead ground squirrel was always worth a milk shake from the greens-keeper, Bob Howell. I soon learned fades, slices, duck hooks, cut shots, draws, worm burners, towering fairway woods and pop-ups needed to clear the trees, and skidded pitches that take one bounce and then suck right back. There seemed no end to the magic that could be performed with a golf club and ball. A drive that bordered on an out-and-out duck hook produced the most distance. This stroke would never win a beauty contest (and it wouldn't prove very useful when I began to play better courses)—it resembled a pitcher's drop curve bouncing out in front of home plate—but it would run forever. In all these fun shots there is not an ounce of swing theory. All involved the empirically attained knowledge of just how to attack the golf ball with the clubhead, hands, and arms.

The deceptively simple drill shown in the photos of figure 53 is the next important step along the road to pure impact. The setup differs

FIGURE 53: LEFT-ARM WEDGE DRILL

a: weight on left foot, ball centered   b: takeaway longer, lower than in stance, left hand ahead of ball for chip shot

FIGURE 53: LEFT-ARM WEDGE DRILL (CONTINUED)

c: left arm straight, right knee braced, forearm rotates, and hinging of wrist begins

d: Weight on inside of right foot, wrist is fully hinged

e: left arm pulling, hips begin to clear, legs driving toward target

f: Descending blow, supinated left wrist clubface square to target, weight on left

FIGURE 53: LEFT-ARM WEDGE DRILL (CONTINUED)

g: clubface still very square, swinging long and low along target line

h: following through, clubface now begins to close well past impact, head still down

from the chip shot drills in that my stance is slightly widened and my feet are a bit more square to the target but still quite open. Frames e and f illustrate that the positions just before, at, and slightly beyond impact are nearly identical to those learned earlier.

These simple drills with the wedge are teaching you skills critical for correct striking of the driver. Until now you've focused on leading with your left hand at impact by eliminating the destructive influence of your right hand and learning to attack the ball with the clubhead coming from an inside path. Now you'll begin integrating these skills into powerful, two-handed shots.

The series of photos in figure 54 show my two hands together on a nearly full pitching wedge swing. As you work now with both hands, try to sense that your left arm is in control of the backswing, relax your right arm and shoulder completely, and keep a very light right-hand grip. This should allow you to make a nice full, unrestricted shoulder turn against your braced legs. In particular, work on waiting to hit the ball until the last instant before impact—and then hit it hard!

Frames e, f, and g illustrate the most essential elements of good ball striking. If you haven't learned to get into this position in the hitting zone with a wedge, you don't have a prayer with a driver.

The next step in overcoming fear of the driver is to begin using the driver, first in an easy-to-execute drill to build confidence and then graduating to the full driver swing. I hope you have had the patience to learn the drills in the last two chapters. Every single golfer I've known with a handicap of 5 or more could benefit greatly from the learning of and periodic return to these fundamentals. The secrets of squaring up the clubface for the power hit are embedded in these deceptively simple-looking drills.

FIGURE 54A, B, C, D: THREE-QUARTER WEDGE DRILL

a   b

c

d

FIGURE 54E & F: INTO THE HITTING ZONE

e: reconnected right elbow

f: late hit, hands lead clubhead

g: weight on left foot

h

FIGURE 54I & J: THREE-QUARTER WEDGE DRILL

i

j

15

Driver
Drills

There are three very good reasons why the driver is frightening:

1. Its shaft is much longer than any other club's.
2. Its loft is significantly less than any other club's.
3. Because it goes farther, the potential for trouble is worse.

Our first driver drill uses a very long tee and a choked-up grip, halfway down to the bottom of the grip handle. The ball is about a foot off the ground. I have constructed the tee from wooden dowel rod, sharpened on the bottom end and drilled at the top to accept a standard tee.

The purpose of this drill is to force you to attack the golf ball from an inside path. The swing plane is flattened by the elevated tee, and this flattened swing plane restricts your right elbow from disengaging very far from your right chest. It's also impossible to swing at a ball in this position without making a decent shoulder turn and getting the clubhead around behind you—both tasks with which midhandicappers struggle. Another training aspect of this drill is that you are virtually forced to correctly reconnect your right elbow to your right side (as shown in figure 55c) and wait for the late hit. I'm sure you'll find it much easier to make solid contact with the driver; you'll be surprised at how far you hit the ball with this choked-down grip and a three-quarter backswing. You may even want to take this long tee with you onto the course for practice rounds to help build confidence. When you first start with this drill, swing easily to get the feel for it. Then, as solid contact becomes the norm, begin to hit the ball harder without taking a longer backswing. This inevitably involves building a little more hand speed on the down-

FIGURE 55: DRIVER DRILL FROM ELEVATED TEE

a: tee ball a foot in the air, choke down

b: three-quarter-length backswing, flat swing plane

c: right elbow reconnected, right shoulder held back

d: square through impact

swing (being careful not to spin out with your hips) and retaining the wrist cock and timing its release.

This simple drill is sort of a miracle treatment for many of the most common ailments of the golf swing. Have you ever noticed how much better you hit your shots on the course when the ball is slightly above your feet? That friendly lie, just like this drill, tends to force you to turn your shoulders, get the clubhead around behind you, and limit how much your right elbow disconnects.

Once learned, this drill should be revisited about once a month for ten to fifteen minutes. In the photos of figure 56, I have sunk the tee down another four to six inches and reduced slightly my amount of choke-up on the grip. This gives the top of my backswing a somewhat more normal position—but again, I must make sure that I turn my shoulders and keep my right elbow pointed at the ground.

In the drill shown in figure 57, I tee the ball three to four inches forward of my normal position and use about a three-quarter backswing. Because the ball is so far forward, I must really drive my legs and hips toward the target as the downswing begins, attack the ball from the inside

FIGURE 56: SECOND-STAGE DRIVER DRILL FROM ELEVATED TEE

a: ball about eight inches in air   **b**: grip choked down halfway

FIGURE 57: DRIVER DRILL, CHASE IT DOWN THE TARGET LINE

a: ball three to four inches forward

b: legs must drive to reach ball

c: late hit

d: club and hands chase down target line

path, and hang on to the late hit. If I don't make these correct motions, the clubhead will reach the bottom of its arc before I reach the ball. This drill of "chasing" after the ball teed forward is a great training exercise for all golfers. It helps you develop the coordination needed to power squarely through the ball and follow through long and low down the target line. Very many golfers end up falling back onto their back foot at the finish of the swing. This drill must be done with an easy swing first; when you've learned the balance and coordination, you can then add more power.

The drill shown in figure 58 will teach you the correct feel in the impact zone with the driver. After taking my normal address position with my driver, I place my hips open to the target and my weight nearly all on my left foot. I then place my upper body and the club into the starting position for the coiling drill. You are going to begin in this position, then coil your shoulders some and cock your wrists a bit (as shown in frame b) without changing your leg or hip or head position.

From the coiled position of frame b you should then pull down with your left arm and thrust forward with the right forearm as you transfer the rest of your weight to your left foot (frame c), making sure to attack the golf ball along the inside path. With the shortened swing of this drill, you should be able to hit the drive about 150 to 180 yards in the air. I think you'll find that you hit the ball very straight and solidly. By starting this drill in the position you're hoping to achieve in the impact zone, you'll eliminate a great number of things that can go wrong with your golf swing. You will be, perhaps for the first time in your life, striking the golf ball with the driver with your weight completely on your left foot at impact.

The final part of this drill is equally useful in improving your balance and coordination. Don't just stop the swing at frame d. Continue on to a full and balanced finish as shown in frames e and f. At the finish you should be standing completely on your left heel, shoulders turned past facing the target, hips facing the target, right knee pointing at the target, and right shoulder touching your chin. As I mentioned before, a golfer's finishing position is like a crime scene. Learn to leave evidence of a good swing.

FIGURE 58: IMPACT ZONE DRILL FOR DRIVER

a: starting position for drill

b: top of backswing for drill

c: into the impact zone

d: through the hitting zone

FIGURE 58: IMPACT ZONE DRILL FOR DRIVER (CONTINUED)

e: transition to the finish   **f**: hold the balanced pose

The three simple drills for the driver shown in this chapter can improve your entire golf game, not just your driving. Spend enough time with each of these drills to get the physical feel of what they can teach. This cannot be conveyed completely with words; you have to sense the correct impact with your muscles and nervous system. Once felt, pure impact is addictive. Hopefully, this book has conveyed an understanding of what is required. Now, with a little work, you can be on your way to driving long and straight.

16

Fifteen-Minute Daily Exercise Set

M ost golfers have neither the time nor the inclination and discipline to make exercise a large part of each day's activities. Golf is not a game in which bulging muscles are helpful. Fluid power and flexibility are the keys to success and longevity. For thirty years I have used the exercises shown here to avoid the back problems that have plagued several members of my family and thousands of golfers.

The fascination with hitting the long ball and the latest generation of drivers combine to entice many players into making an overly aggressive swipe at the golf ball. In so doing they put their bodies into harm's way.

The exercises shown here focus on keeping your spine and hamstrings supple and the abdominal muscles strong. Along with each illustration I have indicated the number of repetitions I do on a normal day. On mornings when I am rushed I may do only half as many repetitions. I also do sets of twenty-five push-ups and eight chin-ups on alternate days, after completing the flexibility exercises.

Rolling out of bed, my lower back hurts every day. Fifteen minutes later, after I complete these exercises, the pain is gone and stays gone all day. I start every day with single-leg rolls, thirty with each leg (figure 59). By the time this first exercise is done, most of the pain is already gone. As

I do these leg rolls, I try to keep my leg as straight as I can, rotating slowly from vertical to horizontal and back.

While none of these exercises is very difficult, if you are starting from scratch with years of accumulated inflexibility, then you must begin carefully and gradually increase the amount of stretch and number of repetitions.

FIGURE 59: LEG ROLLS—THIRTY

a: leg as straight as possible   b: roll slowly, touch ground with toe

FIGURE 60: LEG LIFTS—THIRTY

a: keep toe pointed toward knee   b: push leg behind as you lift

Next come single-leg lifts, figure 60, done lying on your side with your leg as straight as you can manage. Often this exercise is used to tighten up the buttocks, but I find it just as helpful in loosening and strengthening my lower back. It's also a hip stability exercise. As you lift one leg, try to lift it straight up and away from the other leg, on the ground. There's a natural tendency to let this leg swing out in front of you since this makes the exercise easier. To make the leg actually rise up straight, you will have a feeling of pushing it up and behind you.

Next, I do some simple spine stretching. First, lying flat on the ground, slowly push your head and shoulders up as far as possible (frame a) while keeping your hips on the ground. When fully raised in the cobra position, rotate your shoulders slowly as far as possible in either direction, then lower them slowly back to ground.

Now I get into the child's pose position, trying to get my shoulders flat on the ground as close to my body as possible (frame b). Then, in frame c, I tuck my head as close as possible into a fetal position and rock forward and back

FIGURE 61: SPINE STRETCHES—TWO

a: cobra

b: child's pose

c: spine roll

by thrusting my hips forward, pushing off with my knees and then returning to the starting position. Normally I will go through these spine stretching sequences a couple of times, slowly rotating my shoulders back and forth.

Next come crunches, followed by crossover sit-ups. In figure 62a showing the crunches, I put my hands next to my ears rather than behind my head. This prevents me from pulling on my neck during the crunch. These crunches are done fairly slowly—about one every two seconds. In frame b I place the hands behind my head and keep my legs in the coiled and raised position shown. With each sit-up I alternate touching my left elbow to my right kneecap and then vice versa.

The exercise in figure 63 has only recently been added to my routine, taken from Gary Player's *Golf Begins at 50*. This is a more advanced, difficult exercise and should not be attempted out of sequence. Following the other abdominal work, three to five repetitions is about all I can manage. Starting in the position shown in frame a, I slowly coil my left leg while straightening my right, and then reverse. The transitions take a second or two, and I try to hold the extended position for a couple of seconds.

Next come the hamstring stretches, which I think are the most important and difficult of the whole lot. First, I spend about sixty seconds

FIGURE 62: CRUNCHES AND SIT-UPS—FORTY EACH

a: 40 crunches   b: forty crossover sit-ups

in the position shown in figure 64a, alternately touching my toes and grabbing my ankles with my legs as straight and knees as close to the ground as possible. Some yoga moves, such as deep breathing, may help you stretch out. Do not bounce as you stretch for your toes; very gradually increase the stretch. Frame b shows the hamstring stretch: My right

FIGURE 63: CROSSOVER SIT-UP WITH LEG HANG—THREE TO FIVE

a: left shoulder to right knee, left leg straight

b: transition to other side

FIGURE 64: HAMSTRINGS STRETCH

a: gradually toe touch, legs straight sixty seconds

b: hamstrings stretch thirty seconds

knee is flat on the ground, and the bottom of my left foot is against the side of my right knee.

After the other exercises, I can easily touch my toes with the fingertips of both hands. Trying to keep my back as straight as possible and my knee on the ground, I hold this position for thirty seconds, gradually stretching farther until I can touch my toes with the thumbs of each hand simultaneously. Then I repeat with my other leg. Whenever I have any sciatic nerve pain, this exercise seems to really help. If you aren't in the habit of stretching, you will find that you cannot keep your leg straight initially. Don't force it and hurt yourself, but gradually over a month or two eliminate the bend at the knee.

None of these exercises is very difficult. The exact type and number of exercises you do is far less important than simply establishing a daily routine that will help you retain strength and flexibility. There is nothing magic about fifteen minutes, either. When pressed for time, I may shorten the number of repetitions and spend only five minutes, but I can still feel the benefits all through the day.

Index